THE other AMERICA

Teen RUNAWAYS

by
Gail B. Stewart

Photographs by
Natasha Frost

Lucent Books, P.O. Box 289011, Sa

These and other titles are included in *The Other America* series:

Battered Women

The Elderly

Gangs

Gay and Lesbian Youth

The Homeless

Illegal Immigrants

People with AIDS

Teenage Mothers

Teen Runaways

Teens in Prison

Cover design: Carl Franzen

Library of Congress Cataloging-in-Publication Data

Stewart, Gail, 1949–
    Teen runaways / by Gail B. Stewart; photographer Natasha Frost.
        p. cm.—(The other America)
    Includes bibliographical references (p.   ) and index.
    Summary: Presents the stories of teenagers who have run away from
home, the reasons why they did so, and possible solutions to the problem
of runaways.
    ISBN 1-56006-336-X (alk. paper)
    1. Runaway teenagers—United States—Juvenile literature.   2. Child
abuse—United States—Juvenile literature.   [1. Runaways.]   I. Frost,
Natasha, ill.   II. Title.   III. Series: Stewart, Gail, 1949–   Other America.
HV1431.S77   1997
362.7′4—dc20   96-17209
                                                                    CIP
                                                                     AC

Printed in the U.S.A.
Copyright © 1997 by Lucent Books, Inc.
P.O. Box 289011, San Diego, CA 92198-9011

Contents

Katherine dates her problems from the time of her parents' divorce. Her life on the streets has included time in shelters, in squats, and in juvenile hall. Although Katherine claims that a teen can find camaraderie on the streets, one pays a high price in ill health, drug addiction, and fear of being victimized.

A member of the street gang Crips, Greg ran away in an attempt to leave the gang, which he felt was endangering his mother and siblings. Greg's violent past with the gang continues to haunt him as he attempts to establish a permanent home in a new city.

Orlando's life fell apart when his mother died. As his father became more emotionally abusive and addicted to drugs, Orlando left to live with his sister. But he soon found himself on the streets, fending for himself.

When her father's alcoholism and physical abuse became unbearable, Jennifer ran away to lead a life on the streets. In order to survive, Jennifer sold drugs and resorted to prostitution in exchange for places to stay and food to eat.

Foreword

O, YES,
I SAY IT PLAIN,
AMERICA NEVER WAS AMERICA TO ME.
AND YET I SWEAR THIS OATH—
AMERICA WILL BE!
LANGSTON HUGHES

Perhaps more than any other nation in the world, the United States represents an ideal to many people. The ideal of equality—of opportunity, of legal rights, of protection against discrimination and oppression. To a certain extent, this image has proven accurate. But beneath this ideal lies a less idealistic fact—many segments of our society do not feel included in this vision of America.

They are the outsiders—the homeless, the elderly, people with AIDS, teenage mothers, gang members, prisoners, and countless others. When politicians and the media discuss society's ills, the members of these groups are defined as what's wrong with America; they are the people who need fixing, who need help, or increasingly, who need to take more responsibility. And as these people become society's fix-it problem, they lose all identity as individuals and become part of an anonymous group. In the media and in our minds these groups are identified by condition—a disease, crime, morality, poverty. Their condition becomes their identity, and once this occurs, in the eyes of society, they lose their humanity.

The Other America series reveals the members of these groups as individuals. Through in-depth interviews, each person tells his or her unique story. At times these stories are painful, revealing individuals who are struggling to maintain their integrity, their humanity, their lives, in the face of fear, loss, and economic and spiritual hardship. At other times, their tales are exasperating,

4

demonstrating a litany of poor choices, shortsighted thinking, and self-gratification. Nevertheless, their identities remain distinct, their personalities diverse.

As we listen to the people of *The Other America* series describe their experiences they cease to be stereotypically defined and become tangible, individual. In the process, we may begin to understand more profoundly and think more critically about society's problems. When politicians debate, for example, whether the homeless problem is due to a poor economy or lack of initiative, it will help to read the words of the homeless. Perhaps then we can see the issue more clearly. The family who finds itself temporarily homeless because it has always been one paycheck from poverty is not the same as the mother of six who has been chronically chemically dependent. These people's circumstances are not all of one kind, and perhaps we, after all, are not so very different from them. Before we can act to solve the problems of the Other America, we must be willing to look down their path, to see their faces. And perhaps in doing so, we may find a piece of ourselves as well.

Introduction

THE FACTS ABOUT TEEN RUNAWAYS

One boy with greasy blond hair sits in the doorway of a down-town bar, his dirty clothes reeking of marijuana. A fourteen-year-old girl works three blocks over, hooking for a pimp who has threatened to kill her if she tries to leave. A third youth, a seven-teen-year-old, sleeps most of the day in an abandoned warehouse. He has had a cough for six months and is losing weight. He knows he should be tested for AIDS, but the idea scares him.

They are the runaways, part of thousands who leave home each day. Young people under eighteen who can no longer tolerate or are no longer welcome in their homes. One social worker calls them "the soldiers in a million different little wars that are being waged in households all around the nation." In a year up to three million of these "soldiers"—American teens—run away from home. Who are they? Why are they running?"

UNCERTAIN STATISTICS

Most teen runaways—about 69 percent—are white. They come from families of all different income brackets. Some run from small towns, others from large cities or suburbs. The average age is fifteen, say youth workers, and that has dropped from an aver-age age of 17. "That scares me," says one counselor at a Min-neapolis shelter. "I can remember when a seventeen-year-old coming in here off the streets seemed young. Now that kid would be a seasoned veteran compared to most of the kids we've got now. I know of kids being processed [by youth agencies] who are 9 and 10!"

As the average age of runaways has dropped, the numbers of teens leaving home are growing at an alarming rate. In the late 1980s the U.S. Department of Health and Human Services estimated that about half a million teens were running away each year—approximately twelve hundred each day. In January 1996, however, social workers say the number could be three or four times larger than that. Many counselors agree that such statistics are doomed to be low because it is impossible to keep an accurate count of runaways.

"Lots of kids don't seek help from agencies or shelters," says one counselor. "If we don't see them requesting emergency shelter, or help for drug addiction, or any number of other services, they don't get counted. Some don't get counted because they say they're over eighteen. And the saddest ones of all are the ones who never get reported by their parents as having run, so there's no record of them."

"HOW COULD I STAY?"

Although teens leave home for as many different reasons as they have backgrounds, the grim statistics show that the majority are abused. Shelter and youth-resource workers say that between 60 and 70 percent of the runaways they see have been abused either physically or sexually. Counselor Jeffrey Artenstein reports in his book *Runaways*, that about 90 percent of the young people he talked to in his work with the Los Angeles Youth Network had been abused. In one interview, a sixteen-year-old said, "My father beat me several times a week. My mother didn't do nothing about it, so she didn't help me. I'm afraid to take off my clothes in the locker room; what if the teacher sees these bruises? So you tell me—how could I stay there?"

Another girl, Jennifer, reports in this book that she and her sister were molested by their two uncles but that no one in the family would believe their story. "How am I supposed to make them believe [us] when the uncles are grownups and we're kids?" she asks tearfully. "My dad just told me that if they were doing that to me, then I must be deserving it."

Abuse, however common among runaways, is by no means the only reason they leave home. Many feel unable to cope with family problems such as divorce or a death in the family.

"My life turned to crap when my mother remarried," says one teen. "My stepfather was a jerk, always yelling at us kids and really coming down hard on my little brother. My brother Sergio's got asthma, and when you yell at him, he starts breathing hard.

7

But Joe [the stepfather] didn't care. He'd call Sergio names, say whatever he wanted. It made me so mad, but there was nothing I could do about it. And my mother just stood there when Sergio was breathing funny; she just did whatever Joe said."

THROWAWAYS AND PUSHOUTS

Shelter and youth workers are seeing another reason for teens on the streets: they have been encouraged to leave home. Sometimes termed throwaways or "pushouts," these young people have left because their parents have made it clear that they don't want them around.

"My mom is the one who called the cops to get me out," says one girl. "She did the same thing to my sister. And so we end up in juvenile detention, and then shelters, then wherever. And each month we'd hear she was coming to take us home. And then another month would go by, and she wouldn't come. Then it would be like, 'Next month I'll be there.' And on and on. She never came."

Experts say that this story is not unusual. "So many parents are raising their kids alone these days," says one youth advocate, "and they just get stressed out. Bills pile up; they can't make ends meet. And their kids misbehave, maybe get out of line at school, get a little snotty at home. And before you know it, you get a situation that escalates.

"The parents may say, 'Get the hell out of here,' or they may do it in more subtle ways. So the kids leave. And when they get picked up by the cops for vagrancy or whatever, and the parents get a call, it's like, 'Who cares?' I had a kid call me; he said his mother told the police that he wasn't her problem anymore."

IT'S A NIGHTMARE OUT THERE

The life that teens face on the run is fraught with dangers. In many cases it seems that teens simply exchange one horrible situation—their life at home—for another. The young people who return home in a few days or who seek outside assistance for their problems are the lucky ones. Those who remain on the streets, however, are facing dangers worse than almost anything that threatened them at home.

"Oh, you name it," says a three-year veteran of the streets. "I've been raped twice by guys who said they'd be my friend, been shot at, been colder than anyone would believe possible, and had to eat food out of dumpsters. My friend had two miscarriages and finally ended up with HIV. It's a nightmare out there, that's a fact."

Youth advocates agree. They say that young people alone on the streets are the most vulnerable to all the bad things that exist in urban America today. They are, for example, more susceptible to becoming victims of homicide or rape. They are more likely to contract the AIDS virus, too. A shelter in Chicago that offers HIV-screening tests found that almost half of their clients test positive for the virus.

"These kids are underage and undereducated," says one youth advocate. "So their means of survival are pretty limited. Lots of them hook; a girl coming to the city will get swooped up by a pimp pretty quick, and lots of teenage boys do it, too. So they do that, or they deal drugs. And while they're dealing them, they're doing them, too."

"I did lots of panhandling on the streets," says Genevieve, a former runaway from Minneapolis. "I never did drugs or hooked, but we went in the dumpsters behind florist shops and took flowers they'd thrown away. So we sold them for a buck each and made some money. We did dumpster diving for food, too, on occasion, but that was gross. Usually you can go into a Hardee's or McDonald's and grab food off the tables, and you're out the door before anyone knows it."

I'D TELL KIDS NEVER TO DO WHAT I DID

This book does not offer solutions to the problems of runaway teens. Instead, it is a close-up look at the lives of four young people who have found themselves on the streets.

Seventeen-year-old Katherine, is a street-smart teenager who moved from shelter to shelter for years. Upset by her parents' divorce and unwilling and unable to get along with her mother, she preferred life with her "street family."

Eighteen-year-old Greg was a member of a gang in Phoenix, Arizona, who ran thousands of miles from home. Rival gangs had put out a contract on his life, and he feared for the safety of his mother and sisters if he were to stay in Phoenix.

Nineteen-year-old Orlando is a throwaway from Chicago. The son of two doctors, Orlando was unable to cope with either his mother's death or his father's subsequent abuse.

Finally, Jennifer is a fifteen-year-old who lived on the streets when she should have been attending eighth grade. Like many other young people, she was forced to engage in "survival sex" with men in exchange for food and a warm place to sleep.

Their stories are gritty, the language often stark. Each considers himself or herself lucky to be alive, having gone through frightening times on the streets. Although they still are angry about the situations from which they fled, they admit that street life was not a good solution.

"If I could talk to kids right now," says Jennifer, "I'd tell them that they should stay home and work things out, if they could. Or tell someone. And if that someone doesn't believe you, or if things don't change, keep telling another someone, and another. Nothing is worth what I had to do on the streets."

Katherine

"THERE IS A WHOLE WORLD OUT THERE ON THE STREETS, YOU KNOW. . . . IT'S NOT A VERY COOL PLACE MOST OF THE TIME. ANYBODY WHO SAYS IT'S FUN IS WRONG."

She lopes in the front door of the youth center, apologizing for being late. Her long wet hair—a hard-to-describe shade of blonde not found in nature—is plastered to the sides of her head. She carries a bottle of Mountain Dew and a packet of matches.

"Jesus," she says, shaking droplets of water from her oversized black coat, "that rain is brutal. I hate this! I want it to be warm!"

Katherine spots a counselor she knows in the far corner of the room. She shrieks his name and runs over to give him an emotional hug. That accomplished, she returns to her visitors.

"Man, I love that guy," she says, shaking her head. "He is like the coolest guy in the universe. He has helped me so much, I can't tell you."

She arranges herself on an overstuffed chair, long legs up on a coffee table, her black boots almost upsetting the bottle of pop. She swears and steadies the bottle.

"There," she grins, leaning back. "Ready."

"EVERYTHING WAS AN ADVENTURE"

Katherine is, in her own words, "someone who has made a career out of running away." She has been on her own, in varying circumstances, since age twelve.

"It was me and my older sister and my mom and dad," she says. "That's how things were at first, when we were smaller. But that all changed in fifth grade. That's when my parents got divorced. I was—I don't know—eleven, twelve? However old you are in fifth grade, that's how old I was when everything fell apart.

"Before that we were like this suburban family. My dad made lots of money doing different things—real estate, all kinds of stuff. He even installed those little lights on the tops of police cars and made money doing that.

"We had a house in one of the northern suburbs, pretty ordinary as houses go, but it had this *great* yard."

Katherine grins, remembering.

"I guess I was never *in* the house; I was always outside in the swamps behind the house. I was a tomboy, big time, playing in the swamps with the neighborhood boys. We had a lot of fun on the trails. Everything was so cool when we were little kids. Everything was an adventure, the first time we did it. Then it was boring, so we'd do something else. We smoked, we drank, but mostly just playing around, you know?"

Her sister, though fairly close to Katherine in age, was never a part of her adventures in the swamps, she says.

"She was such a little bookworm," Katherine, says, laughing derisively and taking a swig of pop. "There was no way she'd ever come outside with us. No, it was only boys I played with. There were no girls in our neighborhood other than me and my sister. And like I said, she was totally different from me so for me, it was the boys or nobody."

"MY PARENTS HATED EACH OTHER"

While Katherine says that her parents' divorce was traumatic, she admits that the family had deep problems long before her family actually split up.

"Sure, probably the biggest reason I was never home as a little kid—why I spent all my time running around in the swamps—wasn't because I was so outdoorsy. I mean, I liked it, but hey, it wasn't like I was *obsessed* with nature or anything. I just liked being away from the house because my parents fought all the time. I mean, my parents hated each other. If they hadn't gotten a divorce when they did, they probably would have ended up killing each other. Hey, that's no lie."

Katherine remembers her parents fighting about everything.

"No one wanted to be there," she says. "He'd come home from

work and she'd leave. Then she'd come home from wherever she was when he was sleeping. It was one of those numbers. Just stay out of each other's way as much as possible."

She pauses to fish a cigarette out of a crumpled pack and light it.

"I really don't begrudge them that, you know?" she says, exhaling smoke. "I mean, I didn't want to spend time in the house with

Katherine's room walls are covered with the face of Jim Morrison, her "favorite." She likes not only his music, but his intense poetry. "And he's beautiful."

them, either. I totally understood why they had to get out. It was a totally dysfunctional family.

"I'll tell you how screwed up it was," Katherine says ruefully. "In our family everybody had to be on somebody's side. I mean, my dad never liked me. He liked my sister but couldn't stand me—never could find anything about me that he liked. I knew that back when I was six or seven. That's just how it was, and I guess I accepted it. I don't know, I really don't remember.

"But anyway, because my dad had my sister on his side, I was sort of on my mom's side. I'll tell you, I really didn't want to be teamed up with her, because I was usually mad at my mom, too. But I don't know, I've always been kind of soft, you know? I hate seeing someone's feelings get hurt, and she knew that, so my mom would use that to get me on her side.

"I'll give you an example. In fact, this is kind of one of the only warm fuzzy memories I have of my family when I was a kid. We were going to go out for breakfast; I think it was a Sunday, or something. Anyway, my mom was mad at my dad, or something, and she wasn't going to go.

"Well, we got about a block from home, and I started crying. I was yelling, 'We gotta go get Mom, we gotta get Mom!' So my dad turns the car around and we go back to the house. She'd locked herself in the bathroom, and that presented a problem, at least for a minute.

"Both doors were locked—the entrance to the hallway and the one into their bedroom. So my dad picks the lock. And we drag her out: me and my sister each have one of her legs, and my dad's got her from behind. And so we calmly just carry her out to the car. By that time, of course, she's laughing and everything."

Katherine thinks for a few minutes.

"Yeah, that is actually kind of a really nice memory. I always felt sorry for my mom. I was her baby, you know?"

"WHAT A CRUEL MAN"

Even though Katherine did not have a good relationship with her father, his leaving the family was traumatic. It is an event that she still has trouble talking about without emotion.

"I don't know . . . he got a divorce from my mom and then he was gone," she says. "He was living with this woman named Rachel. Now she's his wife. I mean, he traded in my sister, my mom, and me for her. He chose Rachel. That's a plain and simple fact.

"I hate him," she says, her eyes cold. "I'll never forget; we found out that he got remarried because we read it in the newspaper. I'll never forgive him for that. God, what a cruel man. He's really evil.

"At first I tried calling him, when he first moved out. But he didn't want to hear from me, and I guess I wasn't surprised. He didn't like me, like I said. But he really f——ed up my sister by leaving. I mean, when he left us, she suffered. I was pretty much used to him not caring, but she was always his pal, you know? So that was a nightmare for her."

THE FANTASY HOUSE

The divorce was also hard on them, remembers Katherine, for it resulted in a series of moves that uprooted the girls from their schools and friends.

"When the divorce first came through, my mom bought the house she'd always wanted," laughs Katherine. "We called it the fantasy house, since it had everything she'd ever dreamed about: vaulted ceilings, lots of bedrooms, right on a golf course, everything. I guess at first she really made out pretty well financially.

"But then she couldn't pay the bills, and we lost the house. We ended up moving from there to a little house. It was pretty crummy, after the fantasy house, but by that time, everything was crummy, so I didn't really care, you know?"

Katherine says that even though the fantasy house was a nice place to live, her memories of that time are unpleasant.

"It wasn't so much the divorce as it was the fact that my mom started acting very weird," she says. "That was the time that she started getting rid of my sister's and my animals, and we had lots of them. Max was mine, a big white Samoyed [dog]. He was my 'homie'; I just loved him. I used to sleep out in the garage with him when it rained, because my mom wouldn't let him in the house. He got sick, and she got rid of him.

"Then we had Shadow and Sam, two black labs from the humane society. They were cool, too. We loved them. But they just sort of disappeared."

Katherine rolls her eyes and shakes her head.

"Thanks, Mom. That really was nice of you, you know?"

15

Living on the streets didn't offer the stability Katherine needed, not even simple things like a regular meal. "I can make something out of myself. I knew I didn't need anyone else. I proved it."

"EVERYONE KNEW ME"

By the time Katherine, eleven, and her sister started in their new school, both girls were unhappy at home, although it was most obvious in Katherine's behavior.

"My sister wasn't showing anything," Katherine remembers. "I mean, she was screwed up inside like I was, but she didn't let it show. It was just making her crazy on the inside, I think.

"But me, I was mad, and everybody knew it. I started doing really bad in school," says Katherine. "Well, not just in school, just basically f——ing up everywhere, but school was the most dramatic. I hated the place, and I'd skip every chance I got. I even got in trouble for going off on one of my teachers. Jeez, I hated him. Usually, though, I wasn't mouthy. I just didn't show up.

"I also had some real winners for friends," she admits. "I mean, they didn't even know what a textbook was. They didn't care, and at that time, I didn't either. I almost failed, and that was amazing, because I'm pretty smart. But I was in the principal's office every day. He knew me by name, and that was a *big* school! All the secretaries, everyone, knew me. Great, huh?"

"IT WAS LIKE LIVING WITH A WILDEBEEST"

For Katherine it was just a natural progression from misbehaving to running away. She would get into an argument with her mother, and before it was resolved, she would get angry and leave.

"Looking back on it, I can honestly say that I love my mom," says Katherine, "but living with her back then was pure hell. I mean, it was like living with a wildebeest or something. She'd be in my face, constantly talking to me about everything. God, it was annoying. She was trying to be the one in control, and I was busy trying not to let her have any control at all.

"Cleaning is a great example," she says with a laugh. "I mean, she wanted me to clean all the time. I don't clean. I'm not domestic in any way, shape, or form. I don't cook, I don't clean. I won't do s——. I like to order stuff like pizza. I'm good at doing that.

"It's not that I'm lazy, because when I clean, I'm really thorough, really obsessive. I just don't do it very often. But there she'd be, standing in the doorway of my room, demanding that this be dusted or this stuff be put away. No thanks, Mom."

Katherine fiddles with a stray thread on her sweater.

"I think *anybody* standing in my doorway, telling me *anything* would have been an annoyance. See, I'm really a person who needs a lot of alone time. Really, I'm a solitary sort of person. I'm a social butterfly, but I love my solitude. If I don't have a couple of hours a day, I'm not cool.

"But with my mom, it was, 'Katherine, what's wrong?' or 'Katherine, what's the matter?' I hated that. I needed to sort through things on my own. So it just got to the point where I'd say something really angry and leave. Or I just didn't come home at all. I'd show up at midnight when she was asleep. Jeez, it doesn't take a degree in psychology to see that I was doing just what my dad did, right?"

NOTHING SCARY ABOUT RUNAWAY SHELTERS

Katherine's early teenage years were a progression of battles with her mother and running away.

"Sometimes I'd run and I'd end up in a shelter," she remembers. "And sometimes my mom would call the cops on me and make them take me away. Once I got yanked out of school by the police. I guess the teachers thought I was acting crazy. I was taken from home, too. My mom called the police and told them I was unmanageable, so they showed up and took me. I don't know what exactly she was mad at me about. She was good back then at telling lies about me and my sister, so who knows?"

Was it frightening, being taken from her home and placed in a shelter? Katherine laughs and shakes her head.

"I don't think those shelters are scary at all. I mean, it's not like I freaked out the first time my mom tossed me out. I had a blast, I really did. I ended up having a boyfriend at the shelter, and we smoked and just hung out. It was really cool. Hey, I was used to being on my own. I'd been sort of on my own since my dad left, so this was no big deal.

"At a shelter I just looked at it as if I was just under a different roof, still being on my own. I was having fun instead of fighting with my mom. I didn't mind it; I really didn't care. In some ways I guess shelters were less stressful than home."

NOT FOND OF POLICE

Although Katherine has no real complaints about most of the shelters she's visited, her treatment by police is a different story.

"I've met maybe two police officers that were nice. The rest were just pigs," she says, lighting a cigarette. "I'm not afraid of them, and that makes them mad, I think."

She laughs, remembering.

"I think I hit my first cop when I was twelve or thirteen," she says. "I got stopped after dark a block from my house. He told me I was breaking curfew. I tried telling him I was only a block from home. I pointed out my house to the guy.

Katherine's goals are modest: "I don't want to win the Nobel Peace Prize, but I don't want to be a statistic."

"He didn't even listen. He just started putting me in the car, and then I got mad. I started punching him and yelling, 'F—— you, a——!' I'd never do it again, but boy, I was mad. Anyway, he deserved it, because he sexually harassed me—told me he'd tear up the violation if I'd, well, you know."

Katherine waves her hand absentmindedly.

"Anyway, I started laughing. I told him he was a jerk, and no way was I doing anything to him, or for him. I told him I didn't care what he did with his stupid violation. So he took me home.

"The whole thing was so stupid. He brought me home, and five minutes after he left, my mom left, too. And then, as soon as she was gone, I took off again. What a great family, huh?"

I HATED JUVIE

Some of Katherine's running would result in arrests and trips to the juvenile center, a detention facility downtown.

"I don't even remember what the reasons were," Katherine admits. "I know once I was arrested with a bunch of other kids because we were squatting [living] in an empty theater down-town. I mean, it wasn't being used, and there were a bunch of run-aways who used it to sleep in, you know?

"And one other time I remember I was really high, walking around at about three in the morning."

She laughs and shakes her head.

"I looked really scary. I had this long black cloak on, and I was really pale. Anyway, I had a switchblade on me. Hey, I don't care how old you are, or where, but those knives are definitely illegal. And so the cops pulled up, and I knew I was in deep trouble. I wasn't doing anything. I mean, I really wasn't going to hurt any-body or anything, but I guess the little 'po-pos' [police] were scared of me. Anyway, that was the first time I ever had a gun pulled on me. Hey, that was scary, I'll admit it. So that's another time I was taken in for booking and everything."

Katherine pauses, closing her eyes.

"Those were the days when I could just care less about any-thing," she says. "I mean, if I hit a cop, or laughed at them, or called them names, what was the difference? Me, afraid? Of what? No matter what anybody did to me, I didn't care. So they sent me to 'juvie.' That was about as bad as it could get.

"Except the truth was, when I got to juvie, I cared," she says softly. "I hated that place so much. It was so dull, so bland and dreary. No colors, nothing to look at. It just sucked up your brain, it was so bad. I mean, there were books and magazines and stuff, but who can focus on that? All you can think about was, what scheme can I use to get myself free of this place? But otherwise, there was nothing to do. You were just locked up, like a jail.

"The only thing that kept me sane was this big clock tower I could see from my window. It's on the courthouse a few blocks away, and it was lit up at night. That was the only thing that was colorful. And it moved, so there was something. I mean, it moved slowly, but at least it moved, which was more than I was doing, you know?"

"My Grandpa"

Young people are released from the juvenile center either into their parents' custody or to a long-term shelter. In Katherine's case she went from a shelter to the custody of her grandfather, an expe-rience she is still bitter about.

"Every single month my mom was supposed to come and get me," she says. "And every month would go by and it was like, 'I'm not ready, Katherine; I'm not ready yet. I'll take you next month.' But she didn't. I cared, too, because I didn't want to be there with him. He didn't like me. He was verbally abusive to me, always finding fault with me, always criticizing.

"He didn't like me; he didn't like my friends. I hated the school I had to go to when I lived with him . . . just hated everything about that time. But my grandpa—I can't even talk about him without feeling sick. I mean, to this day, I still get sick on Thanksgiving and Christmas. Those are the holidays I spent with him. I get sick to my stomach on those days, really.

"He threatened to kill me. That's true," Katherine says with disgust. "He threatened to raise a hand to me. No, he never hit me. I would have clocked him if he'd tried. That's one thing you have to know about me. I won't tolerate anybody hitting me. I'll never take s—— from anybody.

"People have asked me, 'Why don't you respect your family more?' I tell them that my family is nuts and that they don't respect me. I do not kiss ass to my family members at all. And if any person—I don't care if they're old, woman, man, whoever—if they try to hit me, they'll get their ass kicked. Nobody lays a hand on me without getting dropped."

"I TOOK OUT HIS GUN AND WALKED UP BEHIND HIM"

Katherine says that her hatred for her grandfather was so intense that she actually considered killing him.

"It sounds really horrible now," she says. "But I remember almost getting him one time. I took out his gun and walked up behind him when he was watching television. I stood there a minute, aiming it at his head, not moving a muscle. Then, I don't know, I said, oh the hell with it, I can't do this. He never even knew I was behind him."

Katherine says that she can see the roots of her own family problems in the way her grandfather's family operated, and this angers her.

"My grandpa treated my mom like a princess when she was young," says Katherine. "And he treated his son Mark like s——. That's how I was treated—the same as Mark. It was always the same. My sister was aligned with my dad; she was the princess. I was treated like s——. I remember I complained to my mom about that once, how she was treated like a princess by her father but I was a big nothing to mine. Her answer was, 'Hey, being a princess isn't that great.' I'm like, 'F—— you.' She just didn't get it."

"WE COULDN'T LIVE IN THE SAME HOUSE"

Katherine admits that while life with her grandfather was unpleasant and often painful for her, the alternative—life at home with her mother—was far from happy.

"I'm kind of fuzzy about some of what went on back then," she says. "I know I ran away at one point, and eventually landed back with my mom for a while. But that was awful, too. I learned one thing: that we couldn't live in the same house. Neither one of us could handle it.

Currently, Katherine lives with her best friend and her sister. "Right now we are out of food, and I can't get [my sister] to go with me to the grocery store. We are all so tired."

"Seeing my sister was the only good part, because I'd missed her when I was running away. But she eventually got really messed up inside, like I said before. She'd been holding all that anger in—anger at my father, at my mother for my father leaving. It finally ended up where she started having big fights with my mom and running away just like I had."

Katherine gets an amused look on her face as she remembers.

"You know, she even hit my mom! It was kind of funny. My mom clawed at her and my sister backhanded my mom. I mean, she didn't even hit my mom that hard, but she gasped and overreacted, drama queen that she is. And she called the cops on my sister, told them to take her to juvie.

"Man, I was mad. I went ballistic on those cops. I jumped on the one big fat guy's back and started hitting him. I was screaming and crying, 'You ass, don't take my sister away or she'll kill herself!'"

Katherine shrugs and smiles.

"I don't really know why I said that. I didn't think my sister was suicidal or anything. It just seemed like the thing to say— maybe if I made her seem unstable like that, they wouldn't take her, I guess. But it was no big favor to my sister. Once she got to juvie, they checked her every fifteen minutes, as a suicide watch, you know? Oh, well, I tried!"

A WHOLE WORLD ON THE STREETS

Katherine says that without her sister at home, she had no reason to stay, either.

"Even though I had told the social worker I'd attempt to work things out with my mom, I just couldn't handle being there. So off I'd go, jumping a bus or whatever, and landing back with my friends on the streets. Some were friends I'd made at the shelter; others were just kids I'd met hanging around.

"There is a whole world out there on the streets, you know. It's just so hidden from everything regular people see, you don't even know it's there. It's not a very cool place most of the time. Anybody who says it's fun is wrong. Some of the people are nice. I mean, at one point the people I knew on the streets were closer to me than my family ever was. I really considered them my real family. We stuck by each other, stayed loyal. You really had to have some close friends out there, or you wouldn't make it by yourself."

She is lucky to be alive, Katherine knows now, especially because of the abundance of drugs that she took while on the streets.

"I drank a lot, took lots of drugs," she admits with a smile. "I really don't remember about half of my life, to tell you the truth. I did acid, speed, 'shrooms, pot, lots of weed. No coke. At least, not on purpose. I did find out not that long ago that one of my dealers laced all the drugs he sold. I found that out talking to a drug counselor about the effects I had from the stuff I was using. He said it was probably laced with some pretty dangerous stuff. That's why so much of my memory is gone, man. PCP, heroin, crack—I was smoking all of it without knowing it."

Surprisingly, it was not at all expensive for runaways like Katherine to do drugs.

"You never had to buy it," she says flatly. "People just give it to you. They don't want to smoke alone, or whatever. Or you sleep with a dealer. That's what I did. But like I said, he turned out to be really evil, lacing his stuff like that. I guess he was just really into emotionally screwing up some of the younger girls."

It's Different on the Streets

There were other dangers on the street for Katherine and other runaways besides drugs and drug dealers.

"We had a friend who was really messed up," Katherine remembers. "I know he was almost always on drugs, but I think he had problems apart from that. He once went after my friend and me with an ax. I don't think he was really trying to chop our heads off or anything, but he just flipped out.

"I can't remember why we were even with him. We must have thought he was under control or something. But he really got scary, really fast. I mean, we were running and this ax goes flying over our heads. Just missed us; I'm not lying. It flew into the door, and my friend and I looked at each other and we're like, wow!"

Sometimes it was the basic necessities like food and shelter that were challenges to the runaways, Katherine says.

"There are places you can go to get food free," she explains. "There are even places that specifically help runaway kids. The problem with those places is that you have to check in with them each day at like 3:00 or something like that, if you want to get a meal.

"I was so lazy I just couldn't get up in time to get over there. I mean, I'd get there about seven or something, and that was too late for them. No meal for Katherine, I guess.

"See, the thing was that for kids on the street, time is all different. Most of the time you're up late at night, till four or five in the morning, just screwing around. And that means you usually are getting up late in the afternoon. That's like morning for us."

SQUATS

There are a number of places in the city that runaways know about, places where they can find a place to sleep at night. These are known as squats and might be an abandoned theater, an unused warehouse, or even a warm enclosure between two buildings that is unseen by passersby.

"We used different squats," Katherine says. "The one I used the longest was an old warehouse just north of downtown. You took kind of a skyway to get inside, and that was gross, because you had to step through all this crap—dead pigeons and bird crap about two feet deep.

"There were lots of rooms and long hallways. I remember the place smelled horrible, like a million urinals all together. That's because all the boys peed everywhere, like cats being territorial or something. I have really bad memories of that place, because my best girlfriend from the streets got raped one night. The guy was a jerk; everyone hated him. It happened while she was lying down right next to me in the squat, and I couldn't do anything to help her. She couldn't [help herself] either. She was just crying the whole time, holding my hand. I was just praying the guy wouldn't come after me. He was really big and fat, and someone you didn't want to mess with."

Twice Katherine was on the streets when members of her family tried to bring her home. The first was when her mother came looking for her.

"I was so blown away," Katherine says, with more than a hint of pride. "I mean, here we are, this group of kids who looked scarier than s——. Weird hair, tattoos, the whole thing. And here's my mother, walking right up to me, telling me to come home, asking me where I've been. I mean, you've got to admire her for that, for her guts. God, she had balls that clanked to do something like that, you know?"

Katherine says that she didn't go back with her mother then, nor did she go home when her sister came looking for her.

"That was *really* weird," she says. "My sister was worried that I was going to die on the streets, and she and some of her friends came to bring me home. It happened like this: my homie and I

Katherine sifts through her photo album, which brings back strong memories: "I know that I have seen them already, but pictures capture the essence of what it used to be because nothing is ever the same. The photographs are the window to anything, the window to somebody's life."

had a car and were riding around one day. We were cruising, just chilling and smoking, smoking the fine herb.

"We went uptown and got out, and out of nowhere these four girls come up and attack me. My sister, my old best friend, and two other girls literally picked me up and were half-carrying me down the street. I'm like, 'What the hell! Put me down!' They had me pinned so bad that I was crying. They said they would call the cops; they'd do whatever it took to get me out of there. If they hadn't been holding my arms, I would have hit them."

Katherine says she broke free for a moment and raced away. She found a friend, Micah, who agreed to help her fight off her attackers.

"A Major Brawl"

"It was great," laughs Katherine. "It turned into a major brawl on the street. All of a sudden these other guys, like twenty dudes, they came out of nowhere and start fighting these girls. A big fight, and I'm in the middle.

"My old best friend got one of the boys in a choke hold, and he flipped her and decked her as hard as he could. I crawled out from under their legs and got away. I was in major pain; my clothes were shredded. My face was so bloody I looked like hell. There were cops looking for me—the girls *had* called the cops— and they were looking for these guys that were helping me.

"I was so angry at those girls. I mean, I could understand my sister, because she did it out of love. But the rest of them were asses. One of them had her teeth popped out by my friend Curtis. He was a fighter and wore rings and brass knuckles, so that must have felt pretty painful.

"But she deserved it, as far as I can see. She had no right, no right at all. I didn't want people making decisions for me. I didn't want that at all. I wanted to do things in my own time, my own way. I still am like that. I probably always will be."

Katherine has vivid memories of feeling despair, too. During the time of running away, of being in and out of shelters and the juvenile center, and of being at home, she felt sometimes that there was no hope at all for her.

"A friend of mine gave me a gun," she says. "Well, not really gave it to me; I took it from him, actually. It made me a little more secure having it, although I never really used it. Guns scare me a little. I once played Russian roulette by myself at my dad's, a long, long time ago. I didn't much care if I died or not.

"But on the streets, the gun was insurance. I never fired it, like I said, but I did threaten someone with it. She was a stupid girl who was trying to have sex with my boyfriend. I held it to her head and told her to think again. That's all."

She felt fear, too—especially those times when she was separated from her street family.

"I had gotten out of juvie one time," she says. "My social worker lined me up with this one shelter on the north side. But I was there an hour and I knew I couldn't handle it. I wanted to be with my homies, you know? So I took off.

"I had a dollar on me, and decided to take the bus. I looked really strange, thinking about it now. I had dyed my hair jet black the day before, and I was walking around in my Goth gear. The whole effect was pretty startling, I'm sure. I got on the bus, and it was like a nightmare. I was the only one on the bus. I started getting real paranoid; I could see the driver looking back at me in the rearview mirror.

"I really went crazy when a cop car came driving along next to the bus. I was sure the driver was going to signal him, and he was going to arrest me, and send me back to the shelter."

Katherine lights up another cigarette.

"I've heard those stories—how some shelters deal with chronic runaways. They tell the cops to take your shoes and socks, and they make you walk back to the shelter. In the winter even. That's supposed to be true. It's really cruel; I've known kids that it has happened to. Man, it would never happen to me. I'd be kicking a cop if he tried to take my shoes."

"IT FELT REALLY GOOD TO BE BACK"

Katherine says she jumped off the bus at the first opportunity and was relieved to get back to her street friends.

"I walked and walked and finally ran into a friend of mine, and then we jumped a bus going uptown," she says. "That was pretty cool, because as soon as we got there, I was just rushed by all my friends—my street family. And they were all like, 'Oh, God, where have you been?' It felt really good to be back with them, back away from the shelter, you know?"

However, as good a feeling as it was to be reunited with other runaways, Katherine says that it was a life she could not live forever.

"I was talking to a friend of mine at one point. He just looked at me and said, 'What are you doing? I mean, what the hell are you really *doing*? You've been on your own, and on the streets since what—twelve? thirteen?'

"I guess I listened to him. I guess I was ready to hear that then," Katherine says quietly. "I didn't want to hear it from my mom or from any of the people at the shelters, or the cops, you know? But at that time, he made me look at myself, and I could see I was in trouble.

"I'll be the first to admit my life ain't great now. I mean, there are no happy little fairy tale endings, I know. But I'm off the streets now. No, I couldn't go back to live with my mom; she's a wildebeest, like I said. I do love her. She's put me and my sister through hell, but I love her. I'll never be able to live with her, but from a distance, we can sort of get along. And since my father is such an ass, my mom is like the only parent I've got. I'm living with my sister and my best friend.

"That's the best thing that's happened to me, really, having a best friend. Man, that's one of the greatest feelings. I really care about her. We've been together for a while, but it seems like we've known each other forever.

"Her name is Missy, and I love her to pieces. She really understands what I've been through because she's been there herself. We're very much alike, like soul mates. She just seems to instinctively know when I need help, and she's there. Like the other day, I was so sick that I had to go to the hospital because I was having really major stomach pains. Well, I called her before I left, and no answer. Two minutes later, she walks in, asks me what's going on. I mean, she *never* shows up at that time of day normally. I told her, 'I'm going to the hospital; I'm sick as a dog.' She says, 'Let's go.' Just like that. That's the way we are."

LUCKY

Katherine says that the stomach pains were a result of stress and a case of gonorrhea that she contracted when she was living on the streets. The doctors at the clinic also tested her for AIDS, and that test was negative.

"I guess I'm pretty lucky I came out of there alive. At least I say that now," she says. "I know there is a real possibility I got HIV and the test hasn't picked it up yet. I'm supposed to be retested in six months. I can't think about that now, though; it would make me crazy.

"Sex was a commodity on the streets, and I had relationships. It didn't mean a whole lot. I had three main guys I was with. I was sleeping with all of them during the same period of time. I got pregnant by one of them and lost the baby. It didn't really matter much to me, the miscarriage. I didn't even know I was pregnant until I lost it. I'm glad I didn't have the baby. Man, that's *all* I'd need right now!"

Asked whether her relationships with three boys at the same time caused jealousy, Katherine throws back her head and laughs.

"No, they weren't jealous. Hell, a couple of those guys were bi-sexual and were sleeping with each other! It wasn't like we were building any long-term meaningful relationships, that's for sure. I

Katherine wants to attend the University of Southern California, but doesn't know if she can afford it. She currently goes to a community college. "I love to gain knowledge."

have no feelings any more for the guys I was with on the streets, none at all."

PIPE DREAMS AND TATTOOS

It's difficult for Katherine to look ahead or make plans that are anything more than short-range. Maybe a serious boyfriend some-day, maybe traveling, maybe college.

"It's hard enough for me to do high school," she admits with a grin. "I don't think I'll be lasting very long. I'm in an alternative program, but even that is totally boring. Maybe if we had some re-ally bomb-ass teachers that were good-looking and stuff, maybe that would help. But school is school, and it's hard for me to stay interested enough to show up. Missy's the same way—she just got kicked out of school—she's such a little s——. Hasn't changed her ways, that girl.

"Sometimes I think about being an actor. I'd go out to Califor-nia, where it's not so f——ing cold. I hate it here. I can't imagine living here the rest of my life. I don't know how people do that. Always coats, scarves, that s——. Besides, when you have so many clothes on, your tattoos don't show."

Katherine has several tattoos now but intends to spend some of her next paycheck on at least one more.

"I was into piercing for a while," she says, making a face. "I did my ears, did them up three. But that's boring now. I think tattoos are really bomb-ass. I mean, not on my forearms or anything; you don't want them to always show. I've got a kitty already, a cute lit-tle black one on my leg. And I want a scorpion—I think on the small of my back. And a daisy on my toe. I think that would be just right.

"Anyway, I want to do a lot of things, just different things. I mean, I look at my friends, my street family from the past. So many of them are so strung out, so totally gone—way beyond gone. I don't want to do that anymore. I don't want to be any-where close to that happening again. I want to do something with my life. Some of it's pipe dreams, but who knows what might happen?"

"I'VE BEEN A BAD KID FOREVER"

One of her dreams is to have children someday, a boy and a girl, she says. Katherine has very strong feelings about how children should be raised, and feels that if she ever becomes a parent, she'll be a good one.

"I'm going to be supportive of what my kid does, wants, needs," she says firmly. "I didn't have support in anything I did; nobody cared. I will be there for my kids no matter what they are into, no matter what mistakes they make.

"I mean, I know kids get involved in drugs. I mean, hel-*lo!* Kids drink, they get into drugs, they get involved with sex. I mean, it's going to happen. It's inevitable. Kids are bad, they are naughty, they do things differently from what their parents want them to do. I've been a bad kid forever. I want to be there for my kids. I mean, I don't want them to be little pushers or anything, but I want them to be able to make choices without having their parents hate them or pull away.

Katherine looks sad, strikes a match and watches it burn down to her fingers.

"I feel so bad when I go by the same places uptown where my friends and I hung out. There are all the little kids, wanting to be cool. They are getting abused at home, nobody loves them, nobody cares about them. Or that's what they think. They have nowhere else to go. I drive by there all the time, and it brings me back. I feel for them. But I can't do anything, not really. You can't make kids get off the streets until they're ready. They'll just keep on running, like I did."

Greg

"I STARTED LIVING ON THE
STREETS, SLEEPING ON THE SIDE
OF THE CHURCHES. . . . I'D KICK
BACK WITH MY HOMIES DURING
THE DAY, BUT AT NIGHT, I'D BE
WITH THESE HOMELESS PEOPLE."

As Greg sees things, once a Crip, always a Crip, although he'd be the first to emphasize that he no longer takes part in gang activities. Even so, he still looks the part, with his dark, hooded jacket, sagging blue jeans, and baseball hat.

"I guess I'm still in the habit of wearing the colors," he explains. "I seem to have all Crip colors in my closet—lots of black and blue. To this day, I can't wear red [the color of the rival gang, the Bloods]. I mean, I don't present myself as a Crip, not really. I'm not out there doing stuff with the gang, I don't hang with no gang boys. But it's easier to say I'm still a Crip, still trying to get my respect. People don't mess with you that way.

"But really, you know, I'd like to put all that gang stuff behind me. I mean, that's the reason I ran away from home. I'm a couple thousand miles away from my mother and the rest of my family. The way I see it, if I hadn't run, the gangs would have killed me."

Greg smiles sadly.

"And I got no particular interest in being dead, you know?"

"I WAS ALWAYS IN TROUBLE, BUT NOT BAD TROUBLE"

Greg is a seventeen-year-old black teen. His voice is deep and resonant, although he speaks quietly. He smiles only rarely. Today he

33

is restless, frowning as he stirs a cup of hot chocolate. A cold front, which arrived yesterday, has taken him by surprise.

"I'm not from around here," he says. "I'm not used to this cold weather. I've been living out west, in Phoenix. But I'm really from Kansas City. Lived there until I was eleven. I've never been in a place that gets this cold, and man, I don't know how people stand this."

Are his memories of Kansas City pleasant ones? Greg shrugs.

"In a way it was okay. I was always in trouble, but not bad trouble. I mean, I got in trouble for not doing my work in school, mouthing off to the teacher, stuff like that. But then I flunked first and second grade, and I figured I ought to take school more seriously. It wasn't like I was dumb or anything. I liked reading, stuff like that. I just fooled around.

"I had friends there. After school, we'd just kick it—hang out—you know. We'd play football, hang around at the park across the street from my house.

"We liked fighting, too," he remembers. "It seems like we were always doing that. Someone would be walking through, and they'd want to fight me, or my brother, or one of my friends. It wasn't real serious—I know that now—but it was exciting for us when we were little kids. I remember one time there were like four guys, and they wanted to fight me and my brother."

Greg shakes his head.

"We got whupped, but it was okay. We could handle that. We gave some out, too, you know? My brother and me, we were bad."

"THAT'S WHEN THINGS REALLY SPREAD APART"

Greg's family moved to Phoenix when he was in fourth grade. It was then, he says, that whatever closeness his family had had before simply ended.

"That's when things really spread apart," he says. "Before that, I felt my family was pretty good. It was my parents, my brother, and my two sisters. Things were usually cool, you know. But things changed, really bad."

It was shortly after the family got settled in Phoenix, Greg says, that he received a letter from his father.

"I mean, I never knew that the man my mama was married to wasn't my father. He's my stepfather, but I didn't have any idea about that. But my real father, writing to me—man, that was like a

Hanging out with friends like Coco (right) used to be a normal pastime for Greg, until he met his current girlfriend. He chose her over them because "everything I was doing with them was negative."

bomb. It was completely unexpected. It turns out that he has been in prison since before I was born. He was writing me from prison. He was a big-time drug dealer; he got caught up in it back in Kansas City."

Greg says that the fact that he had a father he knew nothing about upset him.

"Sure, I was mad," he says. "I'd never even known the man. I was just going along, assuming my stepfather was my real father. And none of them told me different—not my mother, not my stepfather, nobody. And then here's this dude writing to me, telling me that he was my father. Not only that, but telling me I had other sisters I didn't even know about, eight of them. They had different mothers, but they'd be half-sisters to me, and I never even knew about them.

"I felt different things about my father, too. I mean, part of it is that I wanted to see him, but another part was that I didn't want to get involved with him, you know. I feel like if he'd really loved me and cared about me, then he wouldn't have done what he did, right? To get himself thrown in jail."

DISOBEYING

In the letter, Greg's father told him about his half-sisters. He told Greg that one of them lived in Phoenix and that he should look her up.

"I met her," says Greg, "and she told me about my father. She said he'd been going to a business school in Kansas City, and that's where he'd met my mama. She graduated, but he got caught with the drugs before he finished and got locked up. My sister had pictures and everything. She knew a lot about what he'd been like. I mean, I was kind of interested . . . who wouldn't be, right? So I made some plans. I kind of wanted to go visit him, get to know him.

"That's when the trouble started. My mama didn't want me getting to know all these new sisters. She really didn't want me getting to know my father. Said she wasn't going to allow that to happen."

Greg says that his mother had shielded him from unpleasant things other times, too, but that he didn't like it.

"I mean, that's what she did. She felt like if there was something happening that was dangerous, or that worried her, she'd just pretend it didn't exist. You couldn't talk to her about those things."

"I WAS DETERMINED"

"It happened in Kansas City when I was young. My cousin died of AIDS. He was gay, and when he got to be about twenty-four, he got really sick. My mama tried to keep me away from it, just like about my dad. I found out he was real sick, and I wanted to go and see him every day. But she's saying, 'You better not let me catch you going over there. I don't care if he's your cousin—you stay away.' That was how she did things, just like this here with my dad."

Greg stares down at his hands and shakes his head again.

"But man, I was determined. I wanted to know the rest of my family—my father and all of them. I mean, I heard her when she said that they were going to be trouble for me, but I really needed to do what I wanted to do. So I went my own way, did things my own way. I went to see my sister, started hanging around with different people. I wasn't listening to my mother, and I *sure* wasn't listening to my stepfather.

36

"I mean, he'd been pretending to be something he wasn't. I told him, my mama can punish me if she wants to, but I ain't taking it from him. He's not my dad; he can't lay a hand on me. I look back now, I know he wanted to be like a male role model for me; he wasn't trying to lie. But I wasn't fully thinking about that. I mean, all I could think of was, he lied to me. I was mad."

INTO THE GANG

It was during this time, when he was twelve, that Greg became a member of the Crips, one of the largest gangs in the United States.

"At first I wasn't really interested," he admits. "I mean, my first week in Arizona I was introduced to these people. I'm eleven at the time, and it didn't really seem like something I needed to do.

"But then a year later I'm hanging around on the streets more, and I get approached by this gang. They were the Crips, but a branch of them called West Side City. There were a lot of gangs in that city, especially Mexican gangs. But West Side City was all races, the biggest one in Arizona.

Until Greg met his girlfriend Heather, he bounced to and from area shelters and friends' houses. Now he lives with Heather, her mother, and her brother. "It feels like home. I feel like we are married already."

"They introduced me to their homies, told me that anything I wanted, they could get for me, you know. They told me if I wanted to be with them I had to be down to fight, down to do whatever. I'm like, that's me, I'm down. From then on, I didn't hang out with nobody that wasn't a Crip."

His time as a member of the West Side City gang is a part of his life Greg would like to forget.

"I did some bad stuff," he says quietly. "I was stealing cars, robbing people's houses. I started messing around with guns, jumping people, chasing people. They called me Baby G—that was my nickname—because I was young, you know, and I did a lot of things to make sure they knew I was down with them.

"The worst thing I ever did? I don't have no trouble remembering it," he says, his voice barely a whisper. "I was in a drive by, I was in the car while my homies were doing it. But the people they were shooting at, they missed. And the bullets went through a wall and hit two shorties [young children], two little babies. I don't know if they died. I don't know if I want to know. I never found out. But it scares me that maybe two little babies had to lose their life because of the people I was hanging with on the south side of Phoenix."

He says that not a day goes by that he doesn't think about the night of that drive by and his part in it.

"Yeah, it haunts me," he says. "I mean, it's an everyday thing, thinking about stuff, stuff that I can't do anything about now. I reminisce; that's about all I do."

"ALL I COULD THINK ABOUT WAS REVENGE"

"I got shot myself, when I was in seventh grade. I remember thinking how scared I was, when the bullet hit me in the shoulder. I was really panicking. But then afterwards, all I could think about was revenge, man—getting the dudes that did that to me. All the fear and the sadness and stuff like that, you don't think about that anymore. Just getting back at those dudes."

There were moments when being in a gang was enjoyable, Greg admits.

"It's a power thing," he says. "If you've never been part of a gang, you wouldn't know. But walking around, knowing that you have a lot of boys that you can depend on, knowing who your friends are, that's cool.

"I remember one time I was locked up for something. I can't remember what it was exactly. You get one hour each day when they let you out of your room to draw, write, watch television, play games, stuff like that. What I did, I got this big old piece of paper and I made a diagram of all my homies—you know, all the boys I was kicking with. It looked kind of cool, you know, lots of names. When I left, I took that with me, hung it up on my wall. That was the decoration of my room. That was all right.

"It got so that everywhere I went in Phoenix, no matter what side of town I was on, some people always knew me. All I had to do was say my name—Baby G—and they knew me. That was cool, you know, being known like that."

He hesitates, then grins.

"Only time it wasn't cool was with the ladies. I mean, I was a player in Phoenix. I had seven or eight girlfriends at one time. But I was so well known that it backfired when I went up to a woman and introduced myself. I didn't know this female, you know. But she's like, 'I heard about you.' She knew I was a player, and she didn't want nothing to do with me. That happened to me three times in a row. I guess you could say I got dissed."

"MY MAMA WAS CRYING AND HITTING ME"

Even though Greg tried to keep his home life separate from his gang life, it was inevitable that the two spilled over into one another. Members of rival gangs, angry about the actions of the West Side City, launched an attack on Greg's house.

"My mama and me, we weren't getting along so well anyway," says Greg. "She had been telling me that I was into some bad stuff, and she knew about the gang. My house got shot up three different times. I wasn't nowhere around any of those times. It was like, I come home and, dang, I'm running in the house to see if the family is all right. My mama was crying and hitting me.

"I hate to see my mom cry, you know. But she couldn't help it, she was so scared and sad and mad at me. My stepfather was telling me I should leave this stuff alone. I remember him saying, 'You must not love your mama and your two little sisters when you are out doing your stuff and these other dudes are coming back on you like that, shooting at our house, our family.' But you know, I do love my mama, and I love my sisters."

Being away from his family is hard for Greg, but he says he has found a family in Heather's family. Greg is very close to Heather's little brother. "I already told him I would be there for him. I look at him as the little brother I never had."

Greg says that his mother begged him to get away from the gang but that he refused.

"We kept moving," he says. "She was trying to get me away from those boys, you know. But I still kept going back. It was like I had to go back. It's the truth when they say about being in for life, not being able to get out of a gang if you want. You either get out by leaving the state or going back on them, cutting them. If you do that, they'll kill you for sure. No way I would do that.

"So we'd move, and then I'd spend even less time at home. I wasn't going to stop being with my boys, that was that. So I'd sort of live on the streets. Sometimes I'd be staying with my homies, but I didn't like that too much. I'd be thinking, I'm invading them, being here all the time. You don't want to impose, you know?"

LIVING ON THE STREETS

"So I started living on the streets, sleeping on the side of churches. I'd rather be doing that. When my mom moved over north one time, there was a big old group of us, hanging at the park, lots of people with no better place to go. I'd kick back with my homies during the day, but at night, I'd be with these homeless people. Oh, some of them were on kind of like the fringes of gangs, you know. But most were just homeless, people without no place to be."

He had no real problem making money then, he says. Stealing more than paid for his food, cigarettes, and liquor.

"If I needed money, I'd steal a bike. Simple," he says, shrugging. "A real expensive one, like a Harro, or a GT. Those are good bikes, you know. They go for seven or eight hundred dollars. Out there on the street, you can get three or four hundred dollars for one of them. It ain't no hard thing to sell them you just take the bike to a bike shop. No questions, just fill out a paper, they give you a check, you go cash the check.

"I was stealing a lot of bikes. Some I kept for myself, most I sold. People are stupid, man. They buy these expensive bikes and then never lock them up. I mean, there was one time when I was walking at night with a friend of mine, and we saw all these bikes, just sitting inside someone's door. You could see them through the window, you know? The door wasn't locked. I just walked up to the door, looked around. I didn't see nobody. I'm looking in, I see one of the bikes is a GT—a real nice red one. I grab the bike, I walk out. Easy."

There were a few close calls, Greg admits, but he never was actually caught.

"I got chased once," he says, with a hint of pride. "They didn't catch me, though. I was back in this neighborhood where I'd already gotten a bike. I grabbed another one, and was taking a 'whiz', just peeing by the side of a garage. All of a sudden this guy in a truck looks at me and comes squealing up. He's like, 'Why you taking my bike—give it back!' He told me to put the bike in the truck.

"So as soon as he gets back in the truck, I lift the bike up, like I'm going to put it in the back of the truck. But instead, I just took off on it. He's chasing me down the street with the truck, and I ended up crashing the bike. I got away, though. Just left the bike and ran."

"I Got to Leave That Stuff Alone"

Another use Greg had for money was buying marijuana. He smoked it a lot, he says, but tried as long as he could to avoid harder drugs.

"I smoked weed, lots and lots of weed," he says. "My cousin in Phoenix, he was from the 'hood, and he started kicking it where I was kicking it, you know. I saw him and a couple other homies of mine smoking that white stuff—coke—you know. I'd never seen that stuff before, and I told them to let me try it.

"My cousin says, 'Naw, I don't want you doing that, Baby G— you're going to get hooked on it.' I told him I wasn't going to get hooked. Anyway, I kept after him to let me try, let me try. So he did."

Greg shakes his head.

"Man, one time, that's all it takes. This was a mixture of crack and coke, you know? And I was hooked, just like he warned me about. I kept doing it, a few other times. But it was funny. That third time, I told myself, no way, man. You are not going to turn on like this anymore. I got to leave that stuff alone.

"It's funny, but I had no trouble walking away from that stuff. But weed? No way. I tried that, but I can't stop. I don't think there's a problem for me. I can handle my high. I just don't want to give it up, because it's fine."

Greg admits that if he hadn't run away from Phoenix, he probably would have become more involved with drugs, both using and distributing.

"That's one thing about gangs that I know," he says. "They are really into that. They get these big old packages of drugs, all kinds. Crack, weed, everything you could name. My cousin was into that really big. He was a big-time boy in the drugs, you know. I was slinging for him for a while, until I got caught one time. I had a 'quad' of weed on me; that's a quarter of a pound. They locked me up for a while for that one.

"But the drugs, hey, that was south central Phoenix. There are two big main streets in south central; it would be like bumper to bumper, cars going north, south, this way, that way—every direction. Low riders, you know, everybody out there, getting high, buying, selling. Just having fun, meeting a lot of fine females. That was all part of it."

In order to save his family, Greg had to leave them. At first he was homesick, but he knew that he was putting his mom and sisters in danger by staying.

RUNNING AWAY

Why did he run away? The question brings Greg's reminiscing up short; his face clouds over as he remembers.

"It got really dangerous there, in Phoenix," he says. "I mean, this other gang had a contract out on me. You know what I'm saying? A contract, as in they wanted me dead. They put the word out on the streets, anybody sees me, they pull the trigger.

"Man, all that slinging I was doing, that caught up with me. My mama was tired of moving everywhere, and I was worried that

43

they were going to go after my family again, and the next time one of them might get hurt, you know, or killed. I couldn't let that happen."

Greg says that when he told some of his fellow gang members that he was leaving town, they were less than understanding.

"Some of my homies, some of my BGs—baby gangsters—who were my age but had lower rank than me, they were like, 'Man, you must not be down with the gang; if you leave you must not really care about the 'hood, you must not be down.' And I'm like, 'No, I'm down with all y'all, you know what I'm saying, but this is something I've got to do.' I told them that if I stayed there I'd be in big trouble. I mean, with the contract out on me by the other gang and the warrants on me that the police had, I was going to be dead or in prison, one or the other. And those weren't the routes I was looking for, I told them."

So last April, Greg left town. He says that when he got on the bus that would take him far away, he had an immediate sensation of calm.

"It was crazy," he says happily. "I got on the bus—it was a three-day trip. I was hanging with this one dude I met on the bus. Neither one of us had any money. I'd given all my money from slinging to my mom, you know. And so whenever the bus would stop somewhere, I'd go in, come back on the bus with my jacket all loaded down with stuff to eat. Doughnuts, candy, stuff like that. We did some dash and dines, too—you know, where you eat and then take off without paying? I don't know why that was so much fun, but it was. It was three whole days, dang! Just kicking back with this new friend, you know. A relief, for a minute."

A NEW PLACE

Greg arrived in his new home [the city is not identified here for Greg's protection] with few plans. He knew that he had a half-sister who lived there, and she was willing to let him stay with her.

"It was strange being here," Greg admits. "The weather was cold, and everything was different than I was used to. The first week I was here, we went to this big mall—my sister and her boyfriend and me. I got grabbed by the police! I was just standing there, didn't do nothing at all. I'm like, dang! This can't be happening to me!

"What happened was this. My sister and her boyfriend and these dudes go running up some stairs at the mall, and I followed them. I didn't know what they were doing; I just didn't want to get separated, because I'd get lost for sure. Next thing, I turn around and I'm getting sprayed in the face with mace. I started swinging. I didn't know what was happening. Anyway, the cops kicked me out of the mall because I was fighting back.

After running away, Greg found he had to keep moving. The shelters had "way too many rules," Greg says. They didn't allow him to do what he wanted, so he never stayed at one for very long.

"Yeah, I was fighting back," he says with a snort. "I wasn't about to let them do that to me. For nothing, man, dang. Anyway, all my sister's friends got kicked out, too."

Greg's troubles in his new surroundings continued when he was attacked by three men outside his sister's house.

"I think one of the dudes was an ex-boyfriend of my sister's," he says bitterly. "I was waiting for my ride, and they came up behind me and . . . ."

He makes a loud cracking sound.

"They hit me over the head with a bottle, you know. I ain't going to lie; I'd been drinking. I must not have felt how bad it was, because I woke up the next morning and there was blood all over the front of me, on my shirt and everything. It was like— man! To this day, if I ever find the three dudes that did that to me, it won't be funny. Dang. It won't even be funny, because, you know, I didn't do anything to them. I mean, to my way of thinking, I didn't do anything to deserve that."

Greg lived for a while with his sister and her boyfriend and later moved in with his sister's mother.

"I had some trouble getting along with my sister's boyfriend," he says flatly. "Mostly, I didn't like the way he treated my sister's little girl, Sharell. I love that little girl; she's like a piece of my own heart. She's two and the most likable kid you'd ever meet.

"Anyway, one time my sister was at a birthday party or something with her friends, and the boyfriend was baby-sitting Sharell. He was getting anxious, you know, wanted my sister to come home from the party, and she wouldn't. Anyway, he hurt that baby, just to get even or something. I think the dude's too jealous, wanting to own my sister.

"But Sharell, she ended up in the hospital, he hurt her so bad. I was so mad I went over there, kicked in the door and whupped him up, you know. I didn't think too much about what I was doing. I just hated that he would do that to a little girl. I mean, she's so small. I told him, you ever lay a hand on Sharell or my sister again, I'll do more than whup you—I'll kill you. And I meant it, man."

"I THOUGHT THINGS WERE GOING GOOD"

It was not long after that when Greg moved in with his sister's mother, an arrangement that would prove to be very hurtful for him.

46

"I had a job and everything," he explains. "It was at this big grocery store, being a bag boy, stock boy, you know? I wasn't getting a lot of money, just $4.25 an hour, but I was working hard. Anyway, I was getting my paycheck, buying myself some new clothes and everything. I thought things were going good, for a minute.

"What happened was this. It turned out that my sister's mother was into crack. She was taking money from me when I wasn't home—cash from my paychecks—and even taking new clothes I'd bought back to the store for refunds! Dang, I was like, what's going on? She was just taking that money and smoking the white stuff, you know? I mean, what got me really mad was that I'd been buying little Sharell some outfits, and she was taking those back, too.

"I tried talking to her, and then I got mad," Greg remembers. "She got mad back and kicked me out. So I ended up on the streets, just for a little while. It didn't take me long to find a shelter—one that lets you stay around if you're a runaway, like I am."

"I HAD NOTHING TO LIVE FOR"

Even though he has gotten used to being on his own, Greg says, there are still things in his life that depress him.

"The shelter's not bad, the one I'm in now," he says. "I mean, it's not a jail or nothing like that. The food isn't the best, but that's okay. And I've been seeing a counselor named Janet, and she's really nice. I like her a lot.

"I guess the worst thing right now for me is feeling hopeless. Not too long ago I was in a hospital because I tried to kill myself. It was about one in the morning, and I had tied my bedsheets together at the shelter and was going to hang myself. The people at the shelter saw me getting ready to do it, and they took me into the hospital.

"The reason? It's hard to explain. I guess I think too much about stuff that's happened to me. I look back on my life and the mess I've made out of everything, you know. My childhood, growing up, the trouble back in Phoenix. And then I think about today, how things are. I remember when I was tying those sheets together, I had nothing to live for, not really." Greg fishes a brown bottle of pills out of his jacket pocket and tosses it on the table.

"That's Prozac. I'm supposed to take that every day. But sometimes I forget in the mornings, and then I have trouble. I mean, even with the pills, I still think sometimes about how it would be better if I were dead. I think about the shooting in Phoenix and stuff, and how I'm just taking up space on the earth. I'm like a zombie, not doing anything. That makes me feel bad. But I'm learning to shake that off, most of the time."

THINKING ABOUT THE FUTURE

Greg says that sometimes he gets energized by making plans, thinking about the future.

"I need to get back to school, I know that. I missed so much school when I was back in Phoenix that I got kicked out. I mean, I missed two whole months in a row. I remember I went back in one day, and they called me down to the office and told me I was kicked out.

"It's funny how that surprised me. I really was shocked—my heart was really beating, you know, because I didn't want that to happen. You think school automatically has to take you, but that isn't true, I guess. So since then, since ninth grade, I haven't been in school."

He tried to register himself when he first arrived from Phoenix, he says, but had no luck.

"They were missing two years of records for me," he says. "Nobody knew where I'd been, and I didn't want them to write back to Phoenix. I didn't want them to know where I was, you know? So they couldn't put me in anywhere. I'm a good reader. The only thing I can't do is math, but I bet I could learn if someone was a good teacher. I know it sounds funny, me saying I'm smart, but it's true. I can speak proper English, too, you know. That's what I used to do. But now I'm out of the habit, because I speak all the slang."

When he's done with school, Greg says he'd like to move away from the city, to a place where it's warm and safe.

"I want to be on my own," he says. "Like I said, the shelter's all right, but they got rules. I mean, they have to. But it would be good not to have to be in by 10:30, or to eat at a certain time, you know?

"I don't know exactly where I'd move. Not Kansas City, not here, not back to Phoenix. And I don't want to go to any big gang place like Chicago or Detroit or LA. That's no good for me, man. I'd like to be away from the guns and all the killing—somewhere on a beach, just chillin'. Man, what a good picture—me just being peaceful!"

Greg says that his long-range dreams include a wife and children.

"I do know that I want to be married for the rest of my life to a girl that I love. And I want to have a son named after me and a daughter named after my niece Sharell. She's the one I bought the outfits for. She has the greatest smile. And she loves me. You should have heard her cry when I left, after I had the argument with my sister's mother.

"I think I'll be the greatest dad in the world. No way I'd be like my dad. I'd never do something stupid and end up in prison. That would be taking my children's father away. I'd never abuse my children, never hurt them. And I wouldn't ever hurt their mother. Man, I don't know how men can beat on their women. That ain't right, and I know that. I told my stepfather once that if he ever hit my mom, I'd kill him. I don't think he ever would, but I wanted him to know how I felt about that."

STAYING FOCUSED

But although dreaming is fun, Greg knows that his life will work out only if he stays focused on the day-to-day things he must do.

Both Heather's mom, Linda (left), and Heather (right), agree that Greg gets more phone calls than anyone in the house.

One of the most important of those things is to remember that he is accountable to himself for all of his actions.

"I tell other people that when they ask me for advice," Greg says vehemently. "I got friends, you know, from the shelter I'm at now, or friends from work. And when they come to me with a problem, it seems like the thing I always say is 'Live your life for *you*.' It seems like a lot of people do what I used to do: worry about making other people happy. They worry what their friends will think, or their girlfriends, or whatever.

"All those people can tell you how they want you to be, and you can listen, but in the end, you know, you have to make your own life. Live your life for you, make it the way you want it. I know I used to worry about my friends, the boys in the gang, you know. They all expected me to act a certain way. But that ain't no good, especially when you think of what I've done, the bad things. That's nothing to feel proud about."

Greg leans forward in his chair, a look of absolute seriousness on his face.

"So that's why I'm going up now. I'm done with going down. I'm worrying about me now, getting my life on the right track. I'll have time to worry about the details of the future later. Lots of people worry too much about the future, but sometimes you have to take it day by day, you know?"

"GANGS AIN'T ME NO MORE"

Greg says that one thing that he knows for sure is that he is through with life as a gang member.

"Gangs ain't me no more. Like I said before, I still consider my-self a Crip, but I'm not living that way. I don't know, maybe that will go away in time. I'm trying hard to lose the gang mentality. I guess I have to do that little by little, just leave it alone.

"But man, it gets to me when I hear these little shorties running around saying they're all this and all that. They are ten, eleven years old, and they are saying they want to be down. It hurts me to hear stuff like that, you know. It makes me want to tell them, 'No, gangs aren't that nice. Gangs are a quick way to end up in prison somewhere, or end up dead.'

"That's no life. Right now I wish I could reach out to all the lit-tle people who think gangs are all that, and tell them gangs are

Greg was reintroduced to the gang scene while hanging out with area gang members. "The only way to get out of a gang is to die," Greg once said. But since meeting his girlfriend, he has broken his old ties.

nothing to mess with. They'll never be the same, once they start. I know that for sure."

"I CAN'T LIVE MY LIFE BEING AFRAID"

Even though Greg has not spoken to his family in Phoenix, he is still hopeful that sometime he can see them again.

"I don't want to see my sister here, or any of them," he says quietly, fiddling with the lace on his boot. "I got no use for all that stuff they're into. I guess I'm really on my own, and that's all right for now. But I'd like to see my mom soon. I miss her. She's got a birthday in February, and I'd really like to be there for that.

"It's risky, but I'd be willing to take a chance. I mean, I know they got contracts out on me. And the police, they've got warrants out for me. But it's my mom, you know what I'm saying? I guess

Greg currently works at a grocery store. He says he doesn't mind the work, but he wants to make lots of money in the future. Next year he wants to return to school and earn his high school diploma.

if anything is going to happen, it will happen. I can't live my life being afraid. That's as good as telling the police that they own me. And there's no one on this earth that owns me, man.

"I ain't afraid of police no more, and that don't mean I'm looking for trouble. I just refuse to be afraid. I used to be, that's true. I mean, back in Phoenix we'd be walking and my homies would say, 'Uh oh, po-pos'—and we'd get all nervous. But now I'm not that way. I just look at them like they're regular people, I guess."

While seeing his mother would give him great satisfaction, Greg says that he knows that he is capable of surviving on his own from now on, if he has to.

"I have some people on my side now, trying to help me. I got friends now, and that's good. I got this one dude named Eric. I met him at a runaway center downtown. Eric's cool. He's an ex-gang boy, got shot up in his eyes. Now he's blind. He's going to get himself a Seeing Eye dog soon.

"I figure I'm luckier than him. At least I can see, you know? He ain't got nowhere to go and can't see. I don't know if I got any-where to go either, but at least I can see where I am. But him and me, we're cool. We're just chillin', talking about stuff we used to do, mistakes we made. We don't want to go back to that life. Maybe we'll keep each other on the honest road. Anyway, I hope so."

Greg grins.

"All I know is, nobody calls me Baby G anymore. 'Greg' is just fine with me."

Orlando

"IT FELT LIKE I'D HIT BOTTOM. . . .
I KEPT THINKING, HAVE I EVER
BEEN IN THIS MUCH TROUBLE?
THE ANSWER WAS NO. I HAD
NOBODY BUT ME."

"I got to tell you straight off," Orlando says. "I'm yawning a lot today, and I don't mean to be rude or anything like that. I'm tired, because I don't get much sleep at all. So don't think it's because I'm bored or anything like that."

That said, Orlando smiles shyly and slumps into an over-stuffed chair. The teen is Puerto Rican by birth but has no trace of an accent. His skin is very dark, his jet-black hair shines. His voice is quiet and gentle, sometimes fading midsentence, becoming inaudible.

"I'm a runaway," he says slowly. "But there's this program here in town that helps people like me get their own place. It's a non-profit thing, supposed to help runaways who want to help themselves be on their own. I got a counselor who has helped me get a little apartment and helps me maintain a budget, get organized.

"It's not for very long, but it helps for now. The program pays some of my rent, and I have to pay the rest. I want to do right, you know. I want to be on my own, because I have nowhere else to go. Anything is better than living at home."

Orlando thinks about what he has just said and smiles.

"Wherever home is, I guess."

"I FELT LIKE I HAD THE PERFECT FAMILY"

Many teen runaways point to tensions within their families as the main reason they leave home. Orlando is no different, although he says that his family life was very pleasant when he was quite young.

"I had no complaints when I was little," says Orlando. "I felt like I had the perfect family. I mean, you hear kids complaining about their moms, their dads. They say stuff like, 'My mom is mean because she yelled at me,' or 'My dad made me take out the garbage, I hate him.' But in my family, things were happy.

"My mother was from Puerto Rico. My father is black; he's American. They met in Arkansas. She was an intern, doing a medical rotation learning to be a cardiologist. My father was an an———."

Orlando snaps his fingers several times impatiently.

"I always have trouble saying it," he says. "What do you call, you know, the person who helps the patient go under before surgery? The anesthesiologist! That's it. My father was an anesthesiologist in the same hospital.

"They met, fell in love, and had me. They didn't get married right away. She had five children already from another relationship back in Puerto Rico, so I was the baby of her six children. My father was willing to take responsibility for all of us, so things must have seemed to my mother like they were working out real well."

MAMA'S BOY

Orlando and his family moved to Chicago after his mother got her degree, and she began her career as a cardiologist in a major hospital there. It was in Chicago that the family began having troubles.

"Things weren't as dandy as they were supposed to be," says Orlando. "My father was real jealous, thought my mom was having an affair with my brothers' and sisters' father. But that was insane—he was dead. But my father didn't believe that; he accused her of two-timing him.

"It was really stupid. I mean, the things he accused her of were outrageous things. How could she be unfaithful with a man who was dead, or who lived thousands of miles away? It was crazy—*he* was crazy. And he got even stranger, believe me."

Orlando remembers that the accusations and the fighting got so bad that his mother and father decided to separate.

"My mother moved back to Puerto Rico then," he says. "She took me, my brother Tawanda, and my other brother Taihon. The

Orlando still gets sad when he thinks about his mother. He was extremely close to her, and after she died, he became estranged from his father.

other kids who were older stayed in Chicago with my father. I can remember hating my father back then, so in a way I was really glad we were going back to Puerto Rico without him.

"See, I was really attached to my mother," he says, his voice almost a whisper. "I guess I was what you call a mama's boy, but I didn't care. I always wanted to be with my mother, every minute. She was born with a bad heart, and she was in pain a lot. So when she was in her room lying down, hurting, I wanted to be next to her.

"My father wasn't a very nice person," he says matter-of-factly. "He tried to keep me away from her all the time. I was about three at the time, and he was determined to keep me away, to punish me for wanting my mom. Sometimes he'd spank me or even lock me in the basement."

Orlando admits he was very focused on his mother back then.

"I know my father and my brothers thought I was really stupid to be so attached to her," he says. "But what they don't understand was that I was the baby of the family. I spent all my time with her, while they were off doing whatever they did. I just made myself part of her, you know? We just bonded together; we stuck together."

BACK TO CHICAGO

Life in Puerto Rico was pleasant for a while, Orlando says. It was nice not having his father shouting and starting fights. It was nice getting to know his mother's relatives in Puerto Rico. But the easy life stopped abruptly when Orlando was seven.

"My mom had a heart attack down there," he says. "It didn't kill her, but she was really weak for a long time. She told me she just couldn't really take care of me for a while, that I should go back to Chicago. My dad came down there and convinced her I needed to go back with him.

"He was trying to get custody of me then," says Orlando bitterly, "but it wasn't because he loved me or anything. It was a power thing. He told her that I needed to spend time with male role models, not just hang around with my mom and my grandmother and everybody down in Puerto Rico. Plus, they fed me a lot down there—the food was really good—and I was really heavy.

"So he kept working on her and eventually scared her into letting me go back with him. She just gave in to him. She told me it would not only be good for me to have more men in my life, but also, because my skin is dark, it would be right to identify with African-American men, like my dad."

Orlando says the idea of moving away with his father terrified him.

"I was afraid of him," he says. "I don't really know why. And a part of it was that I didn't speak any English then. I mean, that's probably why we didn't get along well. He spoke a little Spanish

—just enough to get by. All I knew was that I was going back to Chicago, and I was miserable."

"I'M GONNA MAKE A MAN OUT OF YOU"

Being back in Chicago was even worse than he expected, Orlando says.

"I cried a lot, and I was really nervous," he says. "My dad got mad at me. He kept saying, 'You're a man, you don't need your f——ing mother. You're a pussy, you're a fag. I'm gonna make a man out of you. That's why your mother sent you up here.'

"I didn't really believe that," says Orlando, "but I guess there was a part of me that wasn't sure. It made me so sad, and then I'd end up in a hospital because I was so depressed, crying all the time. They had me on medication, and then I'd get better enough to be released and come home.

"I wasn't happy, though. It sounds really dumb, but I just wanted to be with my mother. I had built her up to be bigger than life, I guess. I was still a little boy, and I worshipped the ground she walked on. If she didn't want me in her life, I wanted to hear it from her, not from my father."

The verbal abuse from his father continued, Orlando says, although today he believes that the name-calling had a positive effect.

"I guess I thank him for it now," he says. "If it hadn't been for him disrespecting me in front of my friends, calling me names like fag and stuff like that, I wouldn't have hidden out in the house by myself so much. And what I did when I hid out was study.

"I got to be really smart in school as the years went by. I read everything there was to read, did extra work none of my teachers even asked for. I took a lot of accelerated classes in English, lots of science. It was all really easy for me. It was so easy I graduated early from high school. I was only fifteen!"

How did Orlando cope with his mother's absence? He looks sad.

"I convinced myself that she died," he says. "Really, at first I was just angry at her for abandoning me, for letting my father have me. I don't remember exactly why I changed. Maybe just to protect my feelings or something. I mean, why would she just leave me, why didn't she come back if she loved me? I couldn't answer those questions, and that made me feel so miserable.

Orlando gets government aid to pay for his apartment but is always saving his paychecks. He hopes to be fully self-sufficient in the near future. He doesn't like relying on other people.

"It's true that she didn't really abandon me. She did write me letters and stuff, but I wouldn't answer them. When she called, I wouldn't talk. I tore up the letters; I destroyed the gifts she'd send on my birthday. That was when I was angry.

"But then, I just handled it like she was dead. It was like she died in Puerto Rico, and that made it easier for me to cope, so I didn't have to wonder how she could love me and send me away with a father who hated me and called me bad names. I told everybody in high school, kids I'd meet, that my mom was dead. Everybody thought that."

REUNITED

When Orlando graduated, at fifteen, from his Chicago high school, his mother made the trip up from Puerto Rico. Her arrival sent him into a panic.

"I was resigned then to being with my dad," he says. "I didn't like him, but I was used to him, you know? I was used to the routine. But her coming back changed things. She and my father worked some things out, and she decided to stay. So I had to deal with her being alive again, and that hurt. At first I didn't even want to be around her. I wanted her to see how miserable she'd made me.

"But it didn't take long until I was reattached to her. I didn't want to forgive her, but I couldn't help it. I really loved her, loved being around her. I went to lectures with her at the hospital and really got interested in medicine. We'd go to the library to do research, and she showed me how to help her do that, too."

Orlando says that things actually were better than they had ever been in their family.

"My father and her were getting along—no yelling and shouting, no big problems," he says. "Things seemed good. My father seemed happier, and he wasn't yelling at me the way he used to. We were like a happy family—something I didn't think would ever happen to us. But I was wrong."

BAD NEWS

"She kept getting sick—chest pains, tiredness," Orlando explains. "She always seemed to lose her energy by the middle of the day, so she'd sleep a lot. One day she went to the doctor, and he told her something really strange. He said that life was like a poker game, and she'd been dealt the s——ty hand.

"I asked her what that meant," he says, yawning. "It seemed like a stupid thing for a doctor to say. She told me that the doctors felt that they could not cure her, that she had coronary artery disease. It was to a point where they couldn't do any surgery because they suspected her heart might collapse. So they couldn't do nothing for her."

Orlando's voice cracks as he tries to stay composed.

"There was one procedure that they *could* try, but it wasn't fool-proof. It was something we'd read about in the library, when we were doing research together. It's where they go through a vein and clear it without doing no surgery on the heart itself. She decided to go for that, to see if that would help her."

The operation seemed to go well at first, Orlando says, but as doctors were preparing to remove life-support machines from her heart, there was trouble.

"They split the main artery," he explains, "and they had to do some emergency surgery, a quadruple bypass. But even that went okay. I remember being really angry, though. I was kind of mad at my mom because she agreed to the risky bypass. That was what we had been trying to avoid. And I was mad at the doctors for screwing the first procedure up. I don't know—I just was angry because everything was moving so fast, and I didn't have any way of controlling it, you know?"

"I WAS REALLY TIRED, DOWN TO MY BONES"

After seven hours of surgery, Orlando's mother was wheeled to intensive care, where doctors could monitor her heart. The staff assured Orlando and his family that things looked good, that the procedure had gone well.

"I couldn't see her right away because my family thought I couldn't take it," says Orlando. "She was all hooked up to machines and everything, and she looked so weak, I guess. But I saw her the next day, and that was hard. I couldn't really touch her or hug her or anything. I just kept asking her how she felt. She couldn't talk very good, but she made me feel comforted.

"I was happy," he says. "I felt like she was going to be fine. I was telling everybody she was going to come out of it. I packed up her clothes. I was sure that in a few days she would come home to start her recuperation. That's what the doctors told us. I knew she'd be weak and be in a wheelchair for a while, but that was okay, just as long as she was there, you know?"

Orlando says that he remembers the night before she was to be unhooked from all her breathing machines. He was happy and excited. It seemed like the first step in her coming home to the family.

"I was doing laundry, getting the house ready," he says. "I went to sleep by eight that night so I could get some real good sleep. I wanted to be awake when we visited my mom the next morning. I was sure tired because I couldn't sleep no other time, I was always so worried. But that night was really different. I was really tired, down to my bones."

THE BAD DAY

When Orlando went with his father to the hospital the next day, he was disappointed, for they were not able to see her.

"The nurses told us she was with the doctors, and it would be a while," he says. "I had some really big flowers for her, and so that was too bad. But we thought, okay, we'll come back tomorrow. But the next day was the same. They said she was with the doctors, and it was a bad time to see her."

Rather than be anxious about this turn of events, Orlando says, he was confident that things were fine.

"I kept thinking that those doctors were good. If she was with them, nothing bad would happen to her. We just had to wait until it was okay to see her, and everything would be all right.

Since the death of his mother, Orlando is wary of hospitals. When he went in for a bad case of pneumonia, the doctors found a heart defect. "They say it's nothing big, and I want to believe them, but it's hard."

"But at two o'clock in the morning, we got this call. All I could hear was this, 'Oh my God, oh my God' from my brothers and sisters. I didn't hear nothing else. She was dead."

Orlando covers his face with his hands for a minute, then speaks very softly.

"That was my bad day, the worst day of my life," he says. "My life totally changed then, from that day, from that exact time. Nothing would be the same after January 31."

THE WORST FEELING

Orlando says that his mother's death sent him into a deep depression, and his father had him committed to a mental hospital.

"It was so strange," he says. "My family would be talking to me at home, but I wasn't hearing them. Everybody was hollering at me, hollering at each other, but I wouldn't notice. I didn't believe that she was dead. I said, 'No!' But they told me it was true.

"It was a feeling that no one could ever, ever, ever, ever explain," Orlando says, shaking his head emphatically. "It was sort of like when it's icy cold outside, and you have a nice thick, warm blanket around you. Then somebody comes up and snatches it away, and you don't have no clothes, no covers. And that's exactly how I felt. I could never get warm.

"I couldn't cry; I didn't. I didn't go to the funeral because I was in the hospital. I missed it all. My head hurt really bad, excruciating pain. I heard people around me, they were talking, but I wasn't able to hear the words, just the sounds of their voices. I felt them touching me, but I didn't really feel it."

He waves his hand in frustration.

"I don't know," he says, "I'm not explaining it too good. I think it's the worst feeling anyone can feel. I didn't feel no hope at all, just empty."

"I FORGOT SHE WAS DEAD"

Orlando stayed in the hospital for three months the first time, then returned when he attempted suicide.

"I don't really remember it too good," he admits. "After I got out the first time, they gave me some medication to take. I wasn't in such good shape. I had lost a lot of weight really fast, and I was depressed and was even hallucinating.

"Anyway, my sister checked on me once when I was back home and found that I'd taken all my pills in one day—like two hundred of them. Then I'd fallen asleep. Well, they rushed me to the hospital and pumped my stomach and readmitted me for a while."

Orlando says that when he got out the second time, things had changed at home.

"My father had kicked all the older kids out of the house except Lamont," he says. "There had been some arguing, some fighting, and they were gone. So it was the three of us."

Orlando rolls his eyes.

"We didn't get along so well. My father was mean again, like he'd been after they'd separated years ago. He was mad at me because I was sad, even though I tried to stay to myself most of the time.

"There was one time when I really upset him without meaning to. See, there was this thing my mom used to do, where she'd tiptoe through the house. We had wooden floors, and sometimes I'd hear the floorboard creak right outside my door, and I'd spot her and we'd laugh.

"Well, after she died, I was in my room and I heard this creak. I forgot she was dead for a minute. I think I was watching television so hard that I just got lost in it. Anyway, I threw open the door, and yelled, 'Boo!' And then I fell down to my knees and I busted out in this loud cry. That's when I cried about my mom for the first time. My father told me, 'Go to your room with that s——, Orlando.' He was mad at me, disgusted, you know?"

But Orlando says the disgust was two-way.

"I came home from the hospital the second time," he says, "and my dad already had a lady friend staying over once in a while. It made me feel strange, that he was already going out, you know? And he went out of his way to be obscene. He said to me, 'Orlando, you know I can find a piece of pussy anywhere; let's see you find another mother.' He had a real ghetto mouth, you know?"

FALLING APART

Orlando soon learned that besides having a new girlfriend, his father also had a new habit—drugs. His dependence on crack and cocaine soon sank the household into virtual poverty.

"We were doing well before all of this," says Orlando. "My mother and father were making good livings, and we didn't want for much. We had stereos, leather coats, nice cars. When I graduated from high school, I'd been given a brand-new red Camaro.

"But he'd gotten into drugs, and he lost his job at the hospital because of it. And there were a lot of strange black guys hanging around the house, acting like they lived there. One time I was in the hall outside my father's room, and when some guys came out, I noticed a real weird smell. I found out later it was crack. He was into it heavy, but he told me it was none of my business."

"I KNEW HE HATED ME"

As it turned out, however, his father's drug habits became Orlando's business.

"He needed money to pay his dealers, and without a job, money was tight. He was selling everything. He sold our furniture, our nice leather sofa and chairs, all our stuff. And my car, that went to the dope man. He owed a lot to the dope man.

"I suppose my brothers and sisters had known about that. Maybe that's why he kicked them out of the house," he says. "I know they don't care much for him. My one sister didn't like him because she saw him hit my mother once. And my other sister, Kim, left on her own before all this other stuff happened, because he tried to molest her once. I felt bad that she left, because she was the sister I was really close to. I could talk to her about things, and she'd understand.

"But anyway, things at the house were awful. I knew he hated me, but he'd put on this big act once in a while. Like when his mother, my grandmother, came to visit, she'd ask him, 'How are you and Orlando getting along?' And he'd say, 'Oh, fine, fine; we're just fine.' But then, after she left, he'd tell me that if I ever got him in trouble with his family, he'd kill me."

Orlando thinks a moment.

"Actually, the way he said it was, 'I'll put you with that bitch'— meaning he'd have me dead, like my mother. That's the way he said it."

One of the worst things about that time, Orlando says, is that there was so little going on in his life except for the constant tension at home.

"I'd always been kind of a loner," he explains. "I had some friends when I was in high school, but not really close ones. I guess I was more comfortable, because of my situation, with just

65

keeping to myself. And the friends I'd had, they lived quite a distance from me. Without a car I wasn't going anywhere.

"The one thing I did was, on Wednesdays I'd go to this gay and bisexual youth group not too far from home. It was like a support group, and I guess I felt pretty comfortable about going to those meetings."

Orlando looks a little embarrassed.

"I got to tell you, I'm gay. I'm sure I'm gay, even though I'm still a virgin. I've never really had sex, although I'm attracted to men, so I guess that's that.

"Being gay is not something we could talk about in my family. My father. . . . Well, like I said before, he was always calling me fag or pussy. Not a real supportive person, if you know what I mean. And my mom—I never really talked about it with her. Not honestly, anyway.

"The closest I ever got was when we were visiting down in Puerto Rico. She was helping me unpack my suitcase, and there was a brochure there from that support group, and she asked me

Orlando likes living alone and says he has always been a loner. Although he has many friends, he spends a lot of time in his apartment, watching television or trying to relax.

what it was. I lied to her; I told her it wasn't even mine. I told her it belonged to a friend.

"She sat down on the bed and told me real seriously that if I was gay, I shouldn't lie about it. I should just tell her. That would have been a good time, I guess. But instead, I acted real offended. I got mad at her and didn't talk to her for a long time during that trip. Looking back, I guess it sounds really mixed up. But I just didn't want her to think that about me. I don't remember if I was embarrassed, or what. But I never talked about it to her. I wish now that I had."

OUT ON HIS OWN

Orlando says that the closest he ever got to having sex with anyone occurred when he ran away from home for the first time.

"I have this friend named Crystal," he says. "Crystal is a guy, but he made money dressing up as a woman and soliciting men, like a prostitute. He convinced me that I didn't have to stay at the house with my father and his friends. He told me there was money to be made, and I thought it sounded good.

"I did like Crystal did, and for a while it worked out for me. I jacked guys off for fifty dollars, did massages, stuff like that. No real sex, if you know what I mean. The money came in, and I was able to get a little studio apartment with a stove and refrigerator, and even a little car. Nothing like the one I'd had, but it ran.

"But after a while, I didn't want to do that stuff no more. I hated actually doing it. I liked the money, I'll admit, but I didn't feel good about it. So I stopped, and then the money stopped, too. I had no rent money, so I had to give up the apartment and start sleeping in my car."

Orlando says that after a while he had a talk with his sister, who advised him to make a truce with his father and ask to move back into the house.

"I worked out a deal with him, where I could store my stuff in the basement. I couldn't have my old room, because by that time all those drug friends of my father's weren't just visiting, they were living there. I stayed down in the basement."

WORSE AND WORSE

The house had looked bad before he'd left, but Orlando was shocked at how much worse it seemed when he returned.

"It was a big place," he says. "Six bedrooms, lots of space. But it was like a tomb. Cold, dirty, no furniture at all. He'd sold everything he could. There was no gas, no heat, no phones. Everything had been shut off because he couldn't pay the bills.

"He was spending a lot of money on drugs then. He still is, I'm sure," says Orlando. "He was getting Social Security because of me—my mom dying and everything—$377 a month. Of course, I never saw a penny of that; he was smoking it up in a couple of weeks. And part of the deal when I came back is that I had to give him money for his drugs—every week."

Orlando says that his room, the basement of the house, was far worse than sleeping in his car.

"I slept on an old soggy couch," he explains. "There were these really big alley rats that lived downstairs with me, so I got me three cats. They weren't much of a match for the rats, let me tell you. Alley rats are big and tough—more than a foot long with long thick tails. They're not afraid of nothing, either. I had a box of doughnuts down there, on the floor next to my couch. One of the rats grabbed the box—the *whole box*—and took it into the wall with him. Man, I still have nightmares about that."

TROUBLE WITH HIS FATHER'S FRIENDS

Besides having trouble getting along with his father, Orlando had frequent run-ins with some of the people living in the house with his father.

"The worst one was a kid named Georgie. He was even younger than me," says Orlando. "He was real mean. He called me fag like my father did, and always was asking me to give him a blow job. I wouldn't, and he'd taunt me. I told my father about it a couple of times, thinking maybe he could tell Georgie to knock it off. But he wouldn't. He said, 'If you're going to be a fag, you've got to take the responsibilities of being a fag.'

"Georgie was trouble for me in other ways. For one thing, he was a thief. He stole a good leather coat from me, as well as a little TV my mom used to use. He'd taken it and sold it. Again, I told my father what was going on, but he accused me of lying. I think he just liked Georgie more."

Orlando gives a short laugh.

"Eventually, he did believe me, though. My father told Georgie to sell the microwave for drug money, and Georgie kept the

68

money. He got mad then, but it didn't last that long. I guess it just shows how deep into drugs my father was—and still is."

He takes a deep breath and looks very uncomfortable.

"I have to tell something, something that happened with Georgie that I'm not real proud of. But I have to be honest, so here it is.

"There was this one gangbanger on our street who had a really nice car. He parked it right outside our house. This guy was really popular; lots of people wanted to be his friend. Anyway, he'd just got new rims put on the wheels of his car and a new radio with huge speakers—really fine.

"Anyhow, that day, Georgie stole the car. Just stole it, when no one was looking. This is the part I'm not proud of: I told the gangbanger about Georgie stealing the car. I mean, I really hated Georgie, which is why I did this. This was going to be the way I got even.

"The guy told me, 'I'll need you to help me. I need you to hold open the door, and I'm going to come back and shoot that guy.' It happened just like that. The gangbanger came to the door and pretended he didn't know me. He asked if Georgie was there; I said yeah. Georgie came to the door, and the guy shot him. Three times, in the stomach. I'd never been around that stuff before, and it really scared me. My father got real scared, too, and ran out the back door."

Orlando leans back and yawns.

"Georgie didn't die," he says softly. "He was in the hospital for quite a while, though, and while he was gone, my father was actually kind of nice to me. But then he came back, and all the bad stuff started back up again—the verbal abuse, the name-calling, all of it. It's too bad, too bad."

RUNNING FAR AWAY

Orlando was feeling that things would never get better at home. He was guilty about his part in Georgie's getting shot, he was angry and hurt by his father's attitude toward him.

"My one sister Kim wrote me from up north, that I should come up and live with her," he says. "But she'd been having trouble herself. She and her boyfriend had been doing lots of crack, and the police had finally taken her kids away from her. She eventually got them back, but I figured she didn't need any company staying there, you know?

"But then she and her boyfriend drove down to Chicago and offered to bring me back with them. I figured they meant it. She knew about the problems with my father, and she understood that I had to get away. They offered me one hundred dollars a month, plus free room and board. All I had to do was stay around each day and baby-sit the kids while she went to work.

"I thought it sounded like a good deal. I did it for a while, but then I talked on the phone to my brother Taihon. He convinced me that I wasn't being smart. He told me to tell Kim that I wasn't going to baby-sit no more, that my main reason for running away from home wasn't to baby-sit. He thought I should get a real job, and that made sense to me."

Orlando shakes his head.

"Plus, to be honest, I wasn't feeling too good about baby-sitting there. They were still doing the drugs, tripping all the time. My job was to keep the kids in the bedroom with me so that they weren't around all that. I remember one time I called my brother, Taihon, and told him that the drug stuff was getting really bad, and to come and pick me up.

"My sister's boyfriend got mad at me, told me to mind my own business, not to be spreading any rumors about him doing drugs. I told him I wanted to stop baby-sitting around there, because I wanted to get a real job."

"I COULD FEEL THE TENSION"

However, Kim and her boyfriend Marvin weren't pleased with Orlando's change of heart. They reminded him of how much he was getting and how little was expected of him.

"They were mad," says Orlando. "They said I'm living the easy life. I guess I didn't want to make them too mad at me. After all, they helped me get out of Chicago. So for a while things went back the way they were, except I knew I wasn't going to stay there very long. I could just tell that they were getting ready to kick me out; I could feel tension. Marvin didn't like me, I knew that. So I started calling around, trying to line up another job, so that I could save up for an apartment.

"But that was hard," he says. "I couldn't work hardly any hours, because Kim and Marvin needed me at home to baby-sit. I was working at this market, just mopping floors. I had a feeling that they were going to get mad at me there at the market, too, be-

In his old apartment, Orlando would sit in the closet to relax. Now that he lives in a studio apartment, he uses his closet for a bedroom. "Sometimes I get kind of claustrophobic."

cause I was always telling them I couldn't work, because of stuff at home."

BAD JUDGMENT

It was at this time, says Orlando, that he did something else that he is ashamed of: he stole money.

"I was being trained at the market to work the cash register, too," he explains. "And so one time I was working there, and no one was around, none of the people that worked there, and I made out three money orders for myself, for one hundred dollars each.

"I was scared. I mean, I was really nervous. And really stupid, because I didn't know there was this big old video camera on me, taking my picture the whole time I was doing it."

Orlando says that he left the store and asked his brother Taihon to help him find his own apartment.

"He asked me how I could afford an apartment of my own," says Orlando. "He said, 'You don't have no money, how can you pay rent?' I just told him that I had some money saved up from Chicago. That was a lie, though. I didn't have anything except those money orders.

"I started feeling real bad then, after we saw the apartment. I had a chance to put a deposit on it, but I just couldn't. Instead, I had Taihon take me to the bank, and I put the money in an account. I didn't know what to do, but I needed some time to think."

Orlando looks sheepish.

"I didn't have a lot of time to do that either, because by the time I got home, Kim was really mad. She's telling me that the police came to the house, that they were going to arrest me for taking money from the store. They had the whole thing on camera, like I said.

"So what I did was I called them back, told them I wanted to turn myself in. I took the money—it was my fault—so I needed to get that straightened out. I went down to the station and met with them, told them the whole story."

"JAIL WOULDN'T BE SO BAD"

Orlando says that his sister warned him that he could go to jail for his crime. However, he insists that he wasn't worried too much about that.

"I had nothing at that point," he says. "I mean, I had no home, I knew that Kim and Marvin were close to kicking me out. Taihon had nowhere for me to stay, and I couldn't go back to Chicago. I didn't want that. So what was left—being homeless on the streets? I mean, at least in jail I'd get three meals a day, maybe get a chance to do some schoolwork. No, jail wouldn't be so bad, not for me."

However, because Orlando confessed and because he was able to give the store back its money, no charges were filed. He was released and went back to the apartment with Kim and Marvin.

"That was the last night I stayed there," he says sadly. "I mean, Marvin was really mad at me. He was mad that I'd stolen that money, because the police ended up coming over. See, there was a restraining order on him so he wasn't really supposed to be there.

Even though Orlando isn't as close to his sister as he used to be, he occasionally talks to her on the phone or grocery-shops with her.

If the police had known he was there, he would have gotten in a lot of trouble.

"So that, and his drugs—I don't know—it all just got bad that night. He kicked in the door and called me all kinds of names. He threw me out, and he and Kim told me that they didn't want to have anything to do with me from that day on. They threw all my stuff outside. It was really cold outside, too.

"I felt real bad for the kids. The oldest girl is seven, and she didn't want me to leave. She kept screaming, 'I'm sorry, I'm sorry!' She thought it was all her fault, all the shouting and cussing."

Orlando says it was a panicky feeling not to have anywhere to go. Everyone he knew was unable or unwilling to help. He had no money to go back to Chicago, even if he had wanted to.

"It felt like I'd hit bottom," he says. "It didn't feel like I could get myself out of this. I kept thinking, have I ever been in this much trouble? The answer was no. I had nobody but me."

"IT WAS HARD EVEN SAYING THOSE WORDS TO A STRANGER"

Orlando stayed a few nights with an old girlfriend of Taihon's. She was on public assistance, however, and wasn't allowed to have people staying with her, so Orlando slept in a storage room in the apartment building.

"It wasn't too bad," he says with a shrug. "Better than lots of runaways have. I'd pile up some towels and blankets in one corner, near the lawn mowers and stuff, and it was okay. In the morning I'd go into her apartment and wash up. But she and my brother had kind of a fight, and I heard them. She was saying, 'Orlando isn't my responsibility; you've got to take him with you.'

"That made me feel real bad. I thought we were getting along okay. I knew while they were arguing that I better get out of there," he says. "I used her phone book and looked in the yellow pages for emergencies, you know, on the front pages? I saw one, First Call for Help, and I called them. I told the lady that answered that I needed a place to stay, because I had nowhere to go. I said that I had been staying with a friend, but she no longer wants me."

He shakes his head, remembering.

"That was such a terrible, terrible feeling. It was hard even saying those words to a stranger."

74

Orlando says that there weren't many agencies open—it was a Sunday. One place the woman at First Call for Help suggested was a shelter for runaways, although it was only for children seventeen and under.

"I told her I was eighteen, though," he says. "I said, 'Don't you have anyplace that will help me?' But she couldn't really find anything, since it was Sunday.

"I decided to call that one shelter anyway, and lie. I told them I was seventeen. They were really nice. They asked where I was, and they said they'd send a cab out to pick me up and bring me to the shelter. I was real excited; I figured things were bound to get better for me."

AN ATTACK OF CONSCIENCE

However, Orlando's feeling of well-being faded as he met the people at the shelter.

"They were so nice, I just had to turn myself in," he says with a laugh. "They were really kind and they were listening to me, and I thought, I can't lie to these people. So I told them I was eighteen, and I was sorry for lying. I said I was sort of desperate, because I had nowhere else to go.

"They told me they'd let me stay one night, but the next day I'd have to leave. But the next day I met this one counselor named Dan. He was really nice. He told me about this shelter for kids my age called Safe House. It was really a good place, he said, but the bad part was that it was pretty hard to get in there, because they never had no openings.

"But it was the strangest thing," he says. "That very day, when Dan called, Safe House had an opening. What a coincidence! They gave me some bus tokens to come out there, but I got lost, so Dan ended up taking me out there."

Orlando says that there were strict rules at the shelter, but he didn't mind at all.

"They made all of us leave every morning by 9:00," he explains. "I think that was so we could either be off to school or maybe look for work. And we had to be in by 8:00 every night— no exceptions.

"There weren't many of us in there. See, it was a regular house, not like an institution like some shelters are. A family ran it. There were three boys; we stayed in the attic. And three girls; they lived on the second floor. The first floor was like a dining room and living room area, where we all could go.

"I really liked it there," he remembers. "It was like a big family. I got to know all the people there real well. We'd cook meals together, rent movies, and watch them together. I liked that a lot. That was pretty much my only experience with a family-type setting that was normal."

"THAT'S WHEN MY LIFE REALLY CHANGED"

The first morning at Safe House was sort of confusing, Orlando admits, since he really didn't have any idea of where to look for work, and he was not registered for school.

"They gave us bus tokens every morning," he says, "and I asked one of the kids at the shelter if he could tell me how to get back to that first shelter I was at, the one where Dan worked. So I hopped a bus and went back there. I met two more counselors there—Janet and Michael—and that's when my life really changed."

The two counselors explained to Orlando that even though he was too old to be a resident at the shelter, he was still eligible to participate in some of their day programs.

"They knew I didn't know anything about what kinds of programs that were offered, and they took me out to lunch and explained some stuff," he says. "Since money was my number one problem, I needed to get a job. We went through the want ads, right there at the restaurant. I told them I had an excellent résumé that I wanted to type, and they typed it for me. I had done well in school and in the part-time jobs I'd had back in Chicago.

"There were two jobs I went after right away," he says: "the Gap and this one gas station–convenience store. And I got them both! I was really, really proud of that. I was working eight hours at one job, then I'd hurry over to the other and work another eight.

"I didn't make it back to Safe House until midnight, and that worried me at first. But they made an exception for me, since I was working two jobs and doing a good job at both of them. I think they could tell I was sincere about wanting to work. They could tell that I wasn't drinking or doing no drugs, and that was important."

"My Best Week Ever"

"That Friday, the first Friday I was at Safe House, I wanted to move out," he says. "I mean, I liked it, but I didn't want to be sponging off people no more. I wanted to move on. I had my two jobs, and Janet and Michael had helped me hook up with a program like I told you about before, where they pay a big chunk of my rent, and I pay the rest.

Though Orlando worked hard at his job, the manager fired him when he needed to be hospitalized for pneumonia. He says he was frustrated by the decision, since he was a good worker and was reliable.

"I told Janet and Michael that I had just enough money from my first paychecks to cover the cash deposit and damage deposit for this one apartment. I really wanted to do it, but I didn't have enough money for food or for clothes for work. They told me not to worry, that they'd set me up with three hundred dollars from their shelter, and another project in town for runaways tossed in three hundred dollars, too.

"That was such a proud time for me. It was my best week ever. New jobs, my own place to stay, plus I even registered for a community college nearby. I felt good, because I was the only person in the history of Safe House to move out after just seven days. I mean, most people stayed the full twenty-one days before they left. But I'd gotten things together, had an apartment, had two jobs. Safe House was proud of me, too. I even got a certificate saying that I had the record for the shortest time stayed there."

When asked whether he has the certificate hanging up in his apartment, he shakes his head, a little embarrassed.

"No, I threw it away," he says. "I really didn't want nothing hanging up saying I was able to leave a shelter in seven days. I mean, I was proud, but I didn't want other people to know, if you know what I mean."

"MAYBE SOMEDAY"

Orlando says that even though being on his own is a little scary, he likes it.

"I keep a clean house—really clean. I'm having a birthday soon, and I think I'll get a cat. They're pretty clean animals, and it would be nice to have the company. I know that I won't be hooking up with my father ever again, or Taihon, or Kim. That part is over, and I can't count on anyone. Where does it get you, anyway?

"I don't really have many friends in town. I had one friend; he was homeless. But he let me down, stole from me, and that was that. I'm used to being alone, though, and it's not a big deal to me."

Orlando taps his front teeth with a pencil, lost in thought.

"I have the reputation, I think, of being a mean, coldhearted person. I don't smile very much. I have walls—you know, I don't let people in very easily. Usually that's good, because I feel uncomfortable around most people.

"But there are times when I feel really abandoned. I know it has a lot to do with my mother's death. I dream about her funeral,

Orlando was excited when he got his cat, because it offers him constant company. The drawbacks are that the cat wakes him up early in the morning and scratches him.

even though I wasn't there. I wake up hollering and have no one to go to, no one to call. I usually handle it by going to the closet and just sitting in there. I spend lots of time there, when I'm scared.

"So I don't sleep much. That's why I'm always yawning during the day. I think more than I should, so the nights are really long. I get really worried about things, and my heart starts beating fast, and I'm afraid. When that happens, either I go to the closet, or I put my coat on and go outside for a while, maybe run over to the little store a couple blocks over. Sometimes just getting cold helps get me less nervous.

"I often wish I had my stuff from Chicago. I had a really nice picture of my mother. Maybe it would be easier to think about her in a positive way if I had a picture, you know? But I can't go back, and they're sure not going to send things to me."

Orlando says that even though he is a runaway, he is working toward a good future for himself.

"I want to do what my mother wanted to do: be a cardiologist. I'm not just interested because she was; I really like medicine. I'm going to take some liberal arts classes so that when I start at the university, all those requirements will be out of the way. I can start right up in pre-med. I think I've got a good chance. I know I'm smart enough; I just need to be strong."

He yawns again and smiles sheepishly.

"I'd give anything for a good night's sleep right now. Maybe someday."

Jennifer

"I KNOW MY SISTERS STARTED RUNNING AWAY AS SOON AS THEY WERE TEENAGERS. . . . I THINK SOMETIMES THAT MY RUNNING AWAY WAS JUST ME FOLLOWING IN MY SISTERS' FOOTSTEPS."

Jennifer's house is small and yellow, set in the middle of the block. On the front porch stands an incredibly large dog, its ears twitching as it stares at the visitors. He is tied up, but the rope seems string thin as it dangles from his collar.

"He's a big baby; he won't hurt you," says Jennifer, tossing a lock of red hair away from her eyes. She unties the animal, who hasn't blinked away once. "He likes company a lot—almost as much as having his stomach rubbed. Come on Smoky, let's go inside and find you a treat."

Jennifer hauls the dog into the kitchen and returns to her guests. In the corner of the room a television is tuned to a daytime talk show, on which kids are talking about hitting their parents. Jennifer turns down the sound and sinks into an overstuffed sofa. She seems shy and ill at ease without the dog to occupy her. She sits stiffly, her hands folded primly in her lap.

It is hard to see this bashful fifteen-year-old girl as she would have been less than a month ago: living on the streets, selling crack, and sleeping with strange men in exchange for a warm place to stay for a couple of nights.

"I HAVE NO IDEA WHY MY MOM DIDN'T KEEP US"

"I've lived in this state my whole life," says Jennifer. "My parents got divorced when I was little, so I don't remember anything about their being together. All I know is that my mom lives in a little town up north, with her boyfriend, and all us kids live here with my dad.

"I've got one stepbrother and one stepsister. They're from my dad's first marriage. They don't live with us now; they're older. But when I was growing up, there were me and my two sisters and my brother living here. Everybody started running away when they got to be teenagers, though. Nobody could get along with my dad, because he's abusive."

She says this last bit matter-of-factly, as though she were reporting his religion or his political party. Asked why her mother did not have custody of the four children if her father was abusive, Jennifer seems vague.

"I know usually the mother gets custody. But my dad's the one. And like I said, he's been very abusive to us. We were with my mom for a while, when I was very small. And then with my grandma, then my aunt. But then we came here, to my dad's, and we've been here ever since. So I have no idea why my mom didn't keep us. No idea."

"HE USED TO COME HOME DRUNK EVERY DAY"

Jennifer says that her father's abusiveness stemmed from his drinking.

"He drank all the time, even though he's better now than he was," she says. "He used to come home drunk every day from work. He'd stop off at the bar and drink with his friends. Then when he came home, he was mean. Sometimes he'd come right home and drink, and on weekends he'd get up in the morning and start right in. All the time, every day."

Did anyone know about how bad the situation was? Jennifer shakes her head.

"Everyone in his family would stick up for him," she says. "No one wanted him to go to jail or anything. There were a few times when if we kids had said something to the police, he would have gotten in trouble, but we never did. Like when we used to have this other dog, and my dad would shoot him in the backside with a BB gun. That made the dog so mean, and he knew it. So once my brother was up on a counter in the kitchen trying to reach a cup, the dog jumped on him and bit him in the face. No reason at all, just out of meanness. My brother was pretty little, and his lip

Her dad abused both Jennifer and her dog. Now, she maintains that her father treats them better.

was all cut up. It was really my dad's fault, you know, because he'd gotten the dog to be mean like that by being cruel to him."

But while the dog was sometimes the one who bore the brunt of her father's rage, the children were a more frequent target.

"One of the things he did sometimes was handcuff us to a shelf or the bed or something, so we couldn't move. Then he'd yell right in our faces, or hit us. I remember one time someone had eaten the frosting off a cupcake, and he was really mad about that. I was the youngest in the family, so I got blamed. He walked over to me and smashed the cupcake all over my face and put me in front of the mirror. He said, 'Boy, don't you look like a clown.'"

Jennifer looks down, embarrassed, as if this had just happened.

"I cried, yeah. Some parents stop yelling or hitting once they get their kids crying, but not my dad. He just kept on going. But I cried, because I was so sad that he would treat me that way. I figured he hated us kids, because that's the way he acted, especially when he was drunk."

NOT THE FAVORITE CHILD

"He was that way to my mom, too, before they got divorced. She told me that. Like he'd be drinking late at night, and then he'd move stuff around the house. Then the next morning he couldn't remember where he'd put something, and he'd get mad and accuse my mom of stealing it. Then he'd beat her up.

"I'm not sure if he beat her up the same as he beat us. With us he used his fists, or a belt. The belt was thick and black, and it had a bunch of holes all over it. It hurt, yeah, hurt a lot."

Jennifer says that even though all of them were abused, her older sister, Heidi, seemed to enjoy favored status with her father.

"He'd punish us for lots of stuff, stuff most kids would just get talked to about, you know? Like cleaning up and doing the dishes, stuff like that. But we'd always get in trouble if we teased Heidi or picked on her. She was his favorite, and if he thought one of us was against her, he'd get furious. He hit us, beat us with the belt.

"Even my mom used to get in trouble on account of Heidi. She told me that when Heidi was little, she'd take forever eating dinner. She didn't like something, or she'd be fooling around, or whatever. Anyway, my mom would make her sit there at the table until she finished eating. When my dad came home from the bar after work, Heidi would sometimes tell on my mom. She'd tell my dad how mean my mom was, making her sit there. So my dad would beat up my mom for doing that to Heidi. She was his favorite, like I said, and you didn't cross her."

DEALING WITH IT

Jennifer remembers the kids in her family dealing with the violence and abuse in different ways.

"I know my sisters started running away as soon as they were teenagers," she says. "They even took me with them a couple of times. They'd disappear, and then eventually they'd come back, or the police would bring them home. Eventually, they moved out, on account of my father. I think sometimes that my running away was just me following in my sisters' footsteps.

"My brother was nice to me at first, when we were smaller. But then he started getting mean like my dad. He was taking after him with the violence. He'd hit me—hard. One time he hit me so hard when I was sitting in the rocking chair that the whole chair tipped

Although she stays at her father's house most of the time, Jennifer visits her mother occasionally. She says that where her mother lives is boring, so she is always drawn back to the excitement of the inner city.

over backwards. I don't remember what I said that he got so mad about. He's just two years older than me."

Jennifer says that as a child she was uncooperative, often doing things she was specifically told not to do. She thinks that this misbehavior might have had something to do with the violence at home.

"I was bad, even in kindergarten," she admits. "We were supposed to buckle up on the bus, but I never would. I just refused. And when we were told never to stick our fingers in light sockets, I did it right away. I think I wanted to get in trouble. Why? I have no idea. But I did it and got shocked.

"My teachers weren't people I could talk to. I never liked school. Even when I was little, I thought it was a waste of time. In a way, going there was a getaway from home, so that much was okay. But I never confided to anyone, never thought it would do much good.

"I told a couple of my friends, but I've learned that most friends you can't even trust. Even close ones. Like I've had some friends of mine come over here and rob my dad, take stuff from my house that was his. Just the other day a friend came over and took a big bag of M & M's and one of my tapes. And the thing is with friends, is that you say something to them about someone else, they just go and spread it around. Then it comes right back to you. No, I don't think it's much good to tell people anything."

A DIFFERENT KIND OF FEAR

In addition to being nervous about her father's volatile temper, Jennifer was afraid of her two uncles—for a different reason.

"They have sexually abused me," she says, looking down at her lap. "They both have, touched me places I didn't want to be touched. It happened like this. When I was over at my aunt's house and they were there, they'd tell me to come in the room and close the door. This was back a couple of years ago, when I was in seventh grade.

"Anyway, they'd ask me to rub their backs, and then they'd start touching me. I knew it was wrong, and I'd walk away. I told them I wouldn't do that anymore, and they got mad at me. That whole thing scared me a lot."

Jennifer says that she tried telling her aunt and her father about the incidents, but neither took her seriously.

Jennifer stands with friends on the steps of a neighborhood house. She finds it difficult to form close friendships because "most friends you can't even trust."

"My dad was really mean. He said, 'That's what you get for being a whore, for letting them do something like that.' And my Aunt Peg, who's my dad's sister, didn't believe me. She asked my uncles about it, but they told her I was lying, so she believed them.

"Plus," Jennifer adds, "I'm not the only one this happened to. Heidi was abused just recently, too. She had borrowed twenty dollars from one of my uncles to get her nails done really fancy. Then when she was over there a couple of weeks ago, he told her that if she came in and sucked their dicks, he wouldn't make her pay back the twenty dollars; he'd just call it even. Heidi didn't tell anybody about it, but I wish she would. I wonder what would happen if she told my dad?"

Jennifer's decision to run away the first time came soon after she was sexually abused by her uncles. However, she says that their behavior was certainly not the only reason she left.

Jennifer gets some makeup tips from a friend. Her friend also gave her a mini-makeover to keep Jennifer from plucking her eyebrows.

"It was mostly because of my dad and his meanness. His drinking was getting worse, and he was calling me names. The night before I left, he was staying up really late, playing his rock and roll music really loud. We'd ask him to turn it down. It was shaking the walls it was so loud. And it was a school night, so we were supposed to be sleeping.

"But he said no, that he was having fun. He wasn't going to turn the music down, and there was nothing we could do about it.

And my uncles were over, too, and he was saying mean things about me being a slut and a whore, saying stuff like that in front of them. He said that I was a big slut and that I was taking after my sisters, who he said were whores."

Early that morning, when the family was still asleep, Jennifer left. She left no note and took few of her belongings.

"SHE UNDERSTANDS HOW I FEEL"

"I went to my friend Kathy's," she says. "She is one of the only people in the world that I can talk to, the only one that believes me when I talk about things. She's a grown-up; she's got kids of her own. I think she's about thirty-two. She's got a son, Tony, who's my age. And she's been through an abusive marriage, so she understands how I feel when I tell her about my father, or my uncles.

"Anyway, I went to Kathy's that first time. I had told her that I might be coming sometime soon, that things were getting really bad at my house. It was wintertime, and, oh, it was so cold."

Jennifer shivers, as if she can still feel the cold.

"Kathy's house isn't too far from here, so it wasn't that far to walk, but it felt like about ten miles. Anyway, Kathy was halfway expecting me. She had told me that she didn't want me there because she could get in trouble with the police for keeping me—there's a law against someone helping a kid run away. But she said I could sleep there for a while, just nothing permanent.

"Well, I stayed at Kathy's for about a month. My dad had looked for me for a while, but once he heard that I was at Kathy's, he stopped looking. He never came there looking for me, never came to get me to come home. He wasn't really a friend of Kathy's, but he sort of knew her because I'd gone to the same school with her kids."

Jennifer shakes her head and rolls her eyes.

"He doesn't like Kathy, he really doesn't. He thinks she has had a bad influence on me. Now if you talk to him, he'll get mad if you mention Kathy's name. He thinks she should have gotten in trouble for letting me stay with her when I was running.

"But really, she's helped me, and lots of other kids. I have this really good friend, Janell, who stayed with Kathy when she ran away. She was having lots of trouble with her mom, and Kathy let her stay there for a while.

"If it hadn't been for Kathy—no kidding—I would have gone crazy. I would have stayed on the streets doing the stuff I did, only I wouldn't have stopped. I might have gotten arrested more, or been sent away to this one work camp up north, like my sister did. It was so important to me, knowing that Kathy cared about where I was."

ON BROADWAY

Jennifer stayed at Kathy's about a month that first time. She would break into her own house through the windows during the day when no one was home to get additional clothes.

"I got along good there," she says. "I like her kids a lot; I think of them as my family. But Kathy told me after a month that it was time I left. She kept telling me that I should go home to my dad's, that it was important to work things out. But I really didn't want to. I wasn't ready to come home.

"I hooked up with these guys I had met over on Broadway— E.Z. and Stubb. They sold crack and told me that I could stay with them as long as I helped them sell. They had an old rundown house, and I had a room there for a while. It was really an awful place, very dirty. It made me feel bad, because there were babies in that house, too. But it was dirty, and there was never any food in the house. Every once in a while E.Z. and Stubb would go out and buy junk food or TV dinners, stuff like that. But never any groceries, real food.

"So I had my little room with a mattress on the floor, and that's where I lived. During the day I walked along Broadway with this one girl, Jennie. She handled the money, and I held the crack. I carried it in plastic bags tucked inside my sock, even in my cheek.

"I never had to approach anyone, because it seemed like everyone knew Jennie. They knew what we were doing, and we had plenty of customers, believe me. We had one guy come up to us with a whole bunch of pizzas, ready to trade us for crack.

"I never really knew where the drugs came from. My job was really just to hold the crack. I supposed that was the lowest job, because I'd be the one to get in trouble if the police found out. But every day, about five in the afternoon, E.Z. and Stubb would come back with more drugs for us to sell. There never seemed to be a shortage, and business was always great."

Jennifer insists that she never was tempted to use the drugs she was selling.

Jennifer stands on the corner where she once sold drugs.

"I've used pot," she says, "and I've done some drinking—pretty heavy, I'll admit. But crack? Never."

She says that she did engage in sex for money while she was staying at the house on Broadway, and that was a time she is not proud of today.

"I did it for extra money sometimes," she says. "I didn't like it

91

while I was doing it. I'd never get myself in that position again, that's for sure. But you've got to understand that that kind of thing happens when you're on the streets.

"I slept with a lot of guys out there. Most of them said they'd give me a place to stay a while if I'd sleep with them. The first time was out in a suburb north of the city. I'd meet up with some guy when I didn't have anyone to stay with. I mean, usually I could find someone, or their car if they had no room inside.

"But if I couldn't find someone I knew, I'd approach guys. This guy up north said, 'Sure, you can stay for a while.' There were actually two guys that first time, and I had to sleep with both of them or I'd get kicked out."

Jennifer smiles sadly.

"It really wasn't worth it at all, though. There were more guys than I can remember, and it was always the same. They'd all promise I could stay a while. But 'a while' turned out usually to be like one night, or two at the most. It wasn't worth it. I didn't think of myself as a prostitute usually, because most of the time the sex was an exchange for a warm place to sleep. It was just while I was on Broadway, with Stubb and E.Z., that I did it for money."

FROM PLACE TO PLACE

The house on Broadway was raided by police several weeks after Jennifer moved in. Luckily for her, she wasn't there at the time, so she was not arrested. Without her income selling crack, she felt she had nowhere to go but back to Kathy's.

"She was kind of glad to see me," says Jennifer. "I mean, she wasn't eager to take me in, seeing as how I'd been reported missing as a runaway by my dad. But she was glad I was still alive.

"I stayed there maybe a month, I'm not sure. But she introduced me to a lady named Carol. She was a neighbor of Kathy's, and she had a baby. Carol told me that if I wanted to baby-sit for her, I could move in and I'd have a place to stay. So that's what I did.

"Carol did some drugs—smoked a lot of pot and did some speed. She didn't do crack or anything. The drugs she did she got from her baby's father. He'd come over a lot; sometimes he'd sleep over there, too. He was selling drugs, so I guess it was real easy for him."

After a month or two, Carol moved to a different part of town, and Jennifer went back to Kathy's again.

"It was just like before," says Jennifer. "She'd tell me to call home, to go back to my dad's. She said she understood that he had a bad temper and that he drank. But she told me that it was better being home fighting those battles than being out on the streets, sleeping with guys, selling drugs. Anything was better than that, she said."

Jennifer and a friend hang out at Kathy's house. Jennifer says it is hard to make good friends, since so many people are "fakey."

Jennifer shrugs.

"She was right; I know that now. But I wasn't ready to go home yet. So I'd stay at Kathy's, even after she started locking her porch so I couldn't get in. But I found a way to break in. I'd come in through the kitchen window late at night when everybody was sleeping. So she'd find me there, sleeping, the next morning.

"Sometimes I ended up going out to Carol's new place, too. I'd ask her if I could do some more baby-sitting, and she'd let me for a while. I don't know . . . I guess I was just managing the best I could. It wasn't always the best, I know now. But then, it was just the best I could."

GETTING CAUGHT

During the time she was running away, Jennifer was obviously not attending school.

"I should have been an eighth grader," she says. "But I wasn't into school then. I had no interest in talking to a counselor, even though I knew they had them at school. Like I said before, I didn't trust those people."

Jennifer, her sister Heidi (right), and Kathy (middle) hang out together at Kathy's house. While she was a runaway, Jennifer spent many nights at Kathy's house, and still visits her close friend.

94

Jennifer bats her hair out of her eyes with an impatient flick of her hand.

"Look, everybody tells you that if you are in trouble, go to your parents, go to a friend, go to someone you trust. So I did that. I went to my father and my aunt when my uncles were doing that stuff. And I told my aunt about my dad's beating us when he drank. So how did that help me, right?

"I just figured that a counselor would be the same way. Anyway, it was my problem, and I was dealing with it the best I could. Since they couldn't make my father stop drinking, how were they going to solve my problem? I worked things out, like I said."

Although Jennifer escaped arrest for prostitution and selling crack, she was picked up occasionally for being under age after curfew. For these infractions, she was usually brought home, although she did not stay long.

"I'd get picked up, yeah," she says. "It was about seven times, maybe eight. The first few times the police would bring me home. Then my dad would wait until the cops left, and then he'd really start in yelling at me, calling me names. He told me how bad I was, how because of me he was probably going to lose his job with the city. He's a sewer maintenance worker—did I say that?

"Anyway, he told me that if I wasn't careful, he was going to tell the police just to lock me up or to send me to that work camp up north that Heidi went to. My good friend, Janell, finally got sent up there two days ago, because she refused to stop running away. So that was what my dad told me."

BACK ON THE STREETS

"But I'd take off again. I'd stay for maybe a night at home, then I'd leave. After being brought home a few times, I started telling the police how bad things were at my house, and how I didn't want to be taken home. They started taking me to a shelter for kids here in the city, and that was way better.

"The cops? I really didn't worry about police one way or another. I mean, I don't like police, just because. . . . I don't know, I just don't like them. Most of them were kind of grouchy; they'd handcuff you like you were some serial killer or something. Sometimes I'd try to bite those guys.

"But there was one cop that I liked. He let me sit up in the front with him, instead of the back seat all locked up. He joked and

While on the run, Jennifer spent time in various shelters, which were an improvement over the streets: The shelters provided good food and, more importantly, a feeling of being safe.

laughed all the way downtown. That was kind of nice. He just treated me like a regular person."

FRIENDLY FACES

Being taken to a shelter was not unpleasant, says Jennifer. It was safe and warm, and there was usually plenty of good food.

"I think the people who ran the different shelters were nice," she says. "After being at one of those for a few days, they'd release me to like an interim care place. The best one of those was run by these older people named Bill and Olga. They were so nice; they were like grandparents to me. They lived in a regular house, so it just seemed really normal.

"Bill and Olga weren't judging anybody. They'd smile a lot, and act interested in you. They trusted you, you know? And they even bought clothes for me, and when I left, they let me take the clothes with me. I really appreciated that."

But after being kept for a week, or possibly two, Jennifer was always released.

"I'd go back to Kathy's sometimes, just to start out again," she says with an embarrassed smile. "And she introduced me to this guy, Herman, who was the brother of her boyfriend. He's a pimp, but she knew I wouldn't whore for him, even though he asked me to. Herman had a wife who was a prostitute, and they had a baby. I baby-sat, and made incredible money—like sixty dollars an hour! He'd let me eat there, too. They had good food at their house, and they were pretty nice."

AN ABUSIVE BOYFRIEND

While staying at Kathy's, Jennifer met an older boy named Tushay. Although she says that she cared about him, she says there was no future in their relationship.

"He was really nice at first," she says. "He'd come by Kathy's and pick me up, or one of his cousins would. He was nineteen, and I had just turned fourteen, so I thought he was really something. He was a singer and had big plans to go out to Las Vegas.

"He even asked me to marry him. He got a ring and everything. At first I thought it was a really good thing, but then it scared me. I couldn't imagine leaving here and going all the way to Las Vegas and getting married. I mean, I had problems with my family and everything, but I guess I always knew I'd come back home eventually. I had problems with my dad, but I wasn't ready to do anything that permanent with Tushay. I mean, maybe things would get better at home. That's what I thought."

Her refusal to accompany Tushay to Las Vegas, however, enraged him. He became violent in ways that she had never seen.

"I told him I was too young," she says. "I tried to explain, but he didn't want to listen. He got really abusive, tried to smother me when I was in bed. He put pillows over my nose and mouth. And he hit me, and even put a gun to my head, told me that I was going to die right there.

"I believed him; I believed that he would kill me. So I stayed with him for a while longer, longer than I wanted to. And there was really nothing for me to do during the day. He wasn't home; he was off doing stuff, working on his singing career. So I'd just wait around."

Eventually, she says, Tushay moved out to Las Vegas without her, probably realizing she wouldn't stay even if he forced her to accompany him.

"He's still out there," she says. "I heard he has a girlfriend now. That's good—she can have him."

OVER AND OVER

Almost a year had gone by, and Jennifer was getting weary of the constant search for places to stay.

"It was getting harder and harder," she admits. "I'd call school friends sometimes, kids I knew might be skipping. I was supposed to be in eighth grade then. Anyway, we'd get together sometimes at night. But when they went home to their houses, there I'd be, with nowhere to go.

"Sometimes I'd still go back to Kathy's. Sometimes I'd lie to kids' parents, telling them that my parents weren't home, that I could sleep over and it was okay. Sometimes it worked; mostly it didn't.

"I called my Aunt Peg a couple of times. She would tell me that I should come home, because I was doing a terrible thing. She said that I was hurting myself, hurting the family. My running was very bad, she said."

Jennifer shakes her head in annoyance.

"But I told her that the family was hurting me, too. I reminded her that my dad was hurting me whenever I'd been home, and that I didn't want to do that anymore. I remember we talked for a good hour that time, and she sort of started listening to me. I think that's when she started understanding my point of view."

"AWAY FROM THE CITY"

The last time Jennifer was picked up by the police, she says, she called her mother up north and asked if she could come up there.

"She hasn't got custody of me, and that was one of the problems," Jennifer explains, "but I thought it might be good to get a change. And maybe that would work for me, being up there away from the city and everything.

"I was supposed to go up just for a visit, just for a couple of days. But then, I'd need some clothes or something, and she'd bring me down to the city to pick stuff up. And then the next thing you know, I'm living there."

One of Jennifer's dreams is to be a singer, but she has trouble performing even for close friends and family on the karaoke machine.

Jennifer says that her mother's house was nice for a while, but it was nowhere near perfect.

"She's got this boyfriend now who's really kind of a jerk. He's really lazy, thinks everybody should clean up after him. He likes to be the boss, and I'm not really comfortable with that. He wasn't abusive, but I got the feeling that he could be.

"See, they have this little puppy they'd just gotten. He was peeing all over, the way puppies do. And so I really gently tapped it on the bottom and told it 'No.' And then he comes up to me all mad, saying that if I ever hit the dog again, he'd start hitting me. I don't know, maybe he would hit me, or maybe that was just talk. But I wasn't hurting the dog; no way would I ever do that to a dog."

Jennifer says that her mother has been more understanding than her father about why she ran away.

"She has been through it herself," says Jennifer. "She worries about me, even though she knows there isn't much she can do. She did tell me never, never to go to my aunt's house when no one is there. She worries that what happened with my uncles might happen again.

"My mom wanted me to stay, I think. But I got kind of sick of being out of the city. I'm a city girl, and I'm used to gangs, and what you might call roughnecks. That's just the city, you know? I don't mind; that seems natural to me.

"And up there, man, it was so quiet, because it's just a little town. There was nothing to do, and the kids are weird. They act stupid, especially the boys. And their voices are so high, they sound like girls! Anyway, I was just sitting around in the house all day up there, so it was boring."

BACK HOME

Jennifer says that after living up north with her mother for a while, she realized she was ready to come back to her father's house. She called her father and asked if she could come home.

"He said yes, that we could try it," she says. "My mom drove me down here, just for a visit, just to see how things went for a while," she explains. "And it went okay. I liked being back home, liked seeing my friends and Kathy.

"But then I would call my mom and tell her that I wanted to stay one more night, one more night. She went along with it for a while, but then she finally told me that if I stay one more night, then I should just live down here.

"My mom's feelings were hurt, I guess. She liked me up there with her, but I think she knew deep down that I didn't belong up there. She worries about me down here, though. There are so many more things to get into that don't exist up where she lives.

"She told me I should make up my mind, that I should think really hard about where I wanted to live. She also told me that

Kathy was not that important; I should learn to get along without her and her kids."

Jennifer shrugs.

"I don't know, though. I called her back and told her that I would stay here, that I was going to live at my dad's. She was sad, but she didn't cry or anything. I think she wanted to, but she wouldn't let herself. And it's not like I won't see her again. I'll be going up there to visit, I'm sure of that.

When Jennifer's phone got disconnected, she used Kathy's to keep in touch with friends. Since she has no mode of transportation, Jennifer sticks close to her neighborhood, but likes to go to the mall whenever she gets the chance.

"One thing that's better here is that my dad is nicer. He has cut way down on his drinking. He's just having a couple of beers after work, but not the hard stuff like he was drinking. He just works all day, has his beers, watches TV and then goes to bed. He says he's tired, and that's okay with me.

"I'm not sure the reasons he cut down. It's not like he went to AA meetings or anything. He's not the type to admit he's got a problem.

"I think one thing is that he watched his kids all leaving on account of his drinking and his abuse. And one time he had really bad chest pains and finally went to the doctor. It wasn't a heart attack like he thought. I don't know what it was, but his doctor told him to cut back on drinking. He's on medication now, too. Maybe that scared him, too."

CALMER TIMES

Whatever the reason, Jennifer is grateful that things are more calm at her house, and she's hoping it lasts.

"It's so quiet now—at least most of the time. It's just me and my dad and my brother, Gary, here. Even Gary is better; he's not hitting me like he used to. I think he's made up his mind to try a little harder, now that I came back.

"Nothing's perfect, though. I mean, my dad still yells at me, still gets mad and calls me names. And when he does that, I get mad back, and yell, say things I shouldn't. But it isn't as much as before. I think everybody is trying."

She says that she plans to enroll in high school and maybe get a part-time job.

"My days were really unstructured when I came home," she says. "I guess they've been unstructured for a while. I just got busy cleaning the house, stuff like that. There wasn't really much else to do, since mostly people I knew were in school. I call my friends sometimes, spend a lot of time over at Kathy's, talking to her. My dad doesn't know that, but that's okay.

"I did this last week," she says, pointing to two shiny gold studs in the right side of her nose. "I did it myself—saved like eighty dollars. I mean, that's what it costs if you have it done. It hurt, yeah. Made my eyes water when I pushed the studs through from the inside. You have to be really careful when you do this, because if you do it wrong, you could paralyze one side of your face."

Jennifer says that for the time being she just wants to be a kid like other kids.

"I am avoiding boys," she says. "I just stay away from them. I had enough of them when I was on the streets. And I'm enjoying eating real food again. I'd lost like thirty pounds. Kathy told me she hardly recognized me when she saw me while I was running. My bones were all sticking out, and I was sick all the time. I had these dark circles under my eyes and everything.

"I'm getting better, though. And, like I said, my dad is better. I know now that what I was doing was hard on him, too. And I'm trying to be better about how I act."

Jennifer's eyes fill with tears.

"There are so many things I wish I could change. I get mad sometimes that my life isn't the way I want it. I watch television, and I see these families all talking and laughing. Their houses are like perfect, and they all dress so nice. The moms and dads—I don't know—they just seem like they love the kids so much, even when the kids do stuff that's bad.

"I wonder why we couldn't have been like that. I wish parents would stay together. I think my parents could have worked things out. It would have been easier on my dad if he didn't have us to raise all by himself. That's a lot of responsibility for one person.

"I don't know for sure if that would have solved anything. But I think so. I just think one parent isn't enough."

Epilogue

In the months since the four people in this book were interviewed, there have been changes in their lives. Greg moved in with his girlfriend and her mother. Although they were concerned that she might be pregnant, tests were negative. He and his girlfriend are now looking for an apartment of their own. He has not started back to school, nor has he found a steady job.

Jennifer still lives with her father. She was arrested two months ago for a theft charge—she had stolen merchandise from a store in a nearby mall. She was found guilty by a judge, and was sentenced to three months of house arrest. Her phone has been disconnected during that time, and she must wear an ankle bracelet with a homing device, so that authorities can make sure that she is always at home.

Katherine's best friend just found out she is pregnant, a fact which clearly bothers Katherine. "Yeah," she says bitterly, "it's not a pleasant surprise. The guy is a jerk, and it's basically ruined [my friend's] life. Katherine herself has a new boyfriend, and the two are planning to move to Atlanta during the summer of 1996. Katherine is getting her high school diploma in August, so the two will leave town shortly afterwards. She has no goals, only to continue working in a restaurant.

Orlando has moved twice in the past six weeks, and now has apparently vanished. All attempts to reach him have failed. His former employer says he has a hunch Orlando might have gone back to Chicago to try and reconcile with his father, but he admits this might be wishful thinking on his part.

Ways You Can Get Involved

THERE ARE MANY WAYS TO BECOME INVOLVED IN THE LIVES OF RUNAWAY TEENS

- Find out about shelters and interim-care facilities in your community. Call them and get information about how they work. Who funds them? What kinds of help do they seek from the people in the community?
- Invite a youth advocate or counselor for homeless youth to speak in your school or group. (Note: Many of the best speakers are themselves former runaways who can share firsthand experiences.)
- Organize a group of your friends or classmates to volunteer at a shelter for troubled or runaway teens. The activity may involve office work, painting, cleaning—anything that needs doing.
- Shelters can always use donations of money. Many shelters and interim-care facilities also have wish lists of donation items— things ranging from games and books to sweatshirts and underwear for their clients.
- Some teens have taken special classes and training sessions, enabling them to work on runaway phone hotlines. Inquire about such phone lines in your area.
- Contact the following organizations for more information about runaway teens:

Children's Defense Fund (CDF)
122 C St. NW
Washington, DC 20001

The CDF is an advocate for children in all kinds of exploitive and abusive situations.

Operation Go Home
PO Box 53157
Ottawa, Ontario
CANADA

This organization helps Canadian teen runaways reunite with their families or assists them in finding an agency that will help them in other ways.

Youth and Child Resource Net
267 Lester Ave., Suite 104
Oakland, CA 94606

This organization helps runaways get off the streets, and assists them in finding help for alcohol and drug addictions.

Each of the following organizations can be a lifeline for a runaway teen, providing information on emergency shelter, food, clothing, health care, and counseling.

Covenant House Nineline
800-999-9999

National Runaway Hotline
800-621-4000

Youth Crisis Hotline
800-448-4663

For Further Reading

Jeffrey Artenstein, *Runaways*. New York: Tom Doherty Associates, 1990. A very readable collection of firsthand accounts of street kids in Hollywood.

Eleanor H. Ayer, *Homeless Children*. San Diego: Lucent Books, 1997. An in-depth look at homeless children, many of whom are runaways.

Patricia Connors, *Runaways: Coping at Home and on the Street*. New York: Rosen Publishing, 1989. Contains a thorough listing of hotlines and agencies that assist runaway youth.

Joan J. Johnson, *Kids Without Homes*. New York: Franklin Watts, 1991. While this book is not specifically about runaways, it gives a vivid picture of the dangers of street life.

Elaine Landau, *The Homeless*. New York: Julian Messner, 1987. Good section on life in a shelter. Helpful bibliography.

Bruce Ritter, *Covenant House: Lifeline to the Street*. New York: Doubleday, 1987. Fascinating, highly readable account of the beginnings of the Covenant House programs.

Index

ABOUT THE AUTHOR

Gail B. Stewart is the author of more than eighty books for children and young adults. She lives in Minneapolis, Minnesota, with her husband Carl and their sons Ted, Elliot, and Flynn. When she is not writing, she spends her time reading, walking, and watching her sons play soccer.

Although she has enjoyed working on each of her books, she says that *The Other America* series has been especially gratifying. "So many of my past books have involved extensive research," she says, "but most of it has been library work—journals, magazines, books. But for these books, the main research has been very human. Spending the day with a little girl who has AIDS, or having lunch in a soup kitchen with a homeless man—these kinds of things give you insight that a library alone just can't match."

Stewart hopes that readers of this series will experience some of the same insights—perhaps even being motivated to use some of the suggestions at the end of each book to become involved with someone of the Other America.

ABOUT THE PHOTOGRAPHER

Twenty-two-year-old Natasha Frost has been a photographer for *The Minnesota Daily*, the University of Minnesota's student newspaper, for three and a half years. She currently attends the University of Minnesota and is studying sociology and journalism.

When not working at the paper or going to school, Frost enjoys traveling. "It gives me a chance to meet different people and expand my knowledge about the world."